CHECK YOUR ENGLISH VOCABULARY FOR

TOEIC®

by

Rawdon Wyatt

A & C Black • London

www.acblack.com

First published in Great Britain in 2006

A & C Black Publishers Ltd
38 Soho Square, London W1D 3HB

A CIP entry for this book is available from the British Library
ISBN-10: 0 7136 7592 6
ISBN-13: 978 0 7136 7592 4

Text typeset by A & C Black
Printed in Italy by Legoprint

A & C Black uses paper produced with elemental chlorine-free pulp,
harvested from managed sustainable forests.

Introduction

This book has been written for anyone who is planning to take the TOEIC®, and who wants to practice and develop their vocabulary. A greater command of vocabulary is one of the key factors that will help you raise your TOEIC® score.

You should not go through the exercises in this book mechanically. It is better to choose areas that you are unfamiliar with, or areas that are of specific interest or importance to you.

Each exercise is accompanied by a full answer key at the back of the book. This key also gives you other information about particular vocabulary items (for example, words with similar meanings, alternative words and expressions, etc.) that are not covered in the exercises themselves.

When you are doing the tasks in this book, look at the instructions carefully to make sure you understand what to do, then read through the text / questions first before attempting the exercises. This is a useful 'skimming' technique that you should also use when you are doing the TOEIC® itself.

We recommend that you have a good dictionary with you, and refer to it when necessary. However, always try to do the exercises *without* a dictionary first, and then use a dictionary to check anything that you are not sure of.

It is very important to keep a record of new words and expressions that you learn, and review these on a regular basis so that they become a part of your 'active' vocabulary. Unless you are taking the TOEIC® Test of Spoken English, the TOEIC® is an exam which tests your language *recognition* skills rather than your language *production* skills. However, if you familiarize yourself with the vocabulary in the book by reviewing it and then trying to use it in your written and spoken English on a regular basis, you will be in a better position to recognize it if and when it comes up in the exam.

No vocabulary book can possibly contain all of the words and expressions that you are likely to come across in the TOEIC®, so it is important that you acquire new vocabulary from other sources. Try to read as much as possible from a different variety of authentic reading materials (books, newspapers, journals, magazines, etc.), and familiarize yourself with spoken English by listening to English-language radio stations and watching English-language movies and television programs whenever possible.

Try to get plenty of exam practice before you do the exam itself, so that you become familiar with the format. There are several books, courses and other publications that will help you. Barron's *How to prepare for the TOEIC®* (ISBN 0 7641 7514 9), which contains lots of helpful advice as well as complete model tests, is particularly useful.

We hope you enjoy doing the exercises in this book and that they help you to practice and develop the vocabulary that you need. Good luck in the TOEIC®!

Contents

For reference see *Dictionary of Law* 4th edition (A & C Black 0-7475-6636-4).

Changes 1

Look at the sentence pairs 1 – 24, then complete the second sentence in each pair with a word or expression from the box so that its meaning is similar to the first sentence. There are some words / expressions in the box that do not fit in any of the sentences. You do <u>not</u> need to change the form of any of the words / expressions.

amended	broaden	build up	considerable growth	constant rise	cuts
deterioration	downsizing	downward trend	dramatic increase	expansion	
fluctuated	general improvement	marked progress	narrow	narrowing	
phased in	phased out	reduce	relaxation	restructure	sharp decline / fall
slipped	steady decrease	streamline	strengthening	tightening up	
upgrade	upward trend	weakening	widening		

1. Last year, 33% of the population worked in secondary industries and 48% worked in the tertiary sector. This year, the figures are 27% and 53% respectively.
There has been a _____ of the gap between those working in different sectors of the economy.

2. Last year, the overseas market accounted for 60% of our sales. This year, it only accounts for about 15%.
There has been a _____ in overseas sales figures in the last year.

3. People can afford to buy more and live more comfortably than they could twenty years ago.
There has been a _____ in the standard of living.

4. Because our company is bigger now than it was two years ago, we need to recruit more employees.
Because of company _____ over the last two years, we need more workers.

5. American travelers abroad have discovered that they can buy more foreign currency with their dollar.
There has been a _____ of the dollar.

6. It is now much harder to import goods into the country than it was a few years ago.
There has been a _____ of border controls for imports.

7. In 2002 inflation was running at about 4%, in 2003 it was 4.5%, in 2004 it was 5% and in 2005 it was 5.5%.
Between 2002 and 2005, there was a _____ in the rate of inflation.

8. Last year, the company employed 200 people. This year it now has over 1000 employees.
There has been a _____ in the number of employees working for the company.

9. Unemployment figures have dropped by about 2% every year for the last four years.
There has been a _____ in unemployment figures over the last four years.

10. Over the next few years, some management positions in the company will be gradually removed.
Some management positions will be _____ over the next few years.

1

For reference see *Easier English Intermediate Dictionary* (0-7475-6989-4).

11. Because of forecasts for high demand in the future, we need to increase our stocks.
We need to _____ our stocks to cope with future demand.

12. The government will spend less on the welfare system next year.
There are going to be _____ in welfare spending next year.

13. Public services are less reliable now than they were five years ago.
There has been a _____ in public services reliability over the last five years.

14. Nowadays, more and more people are traveling abroad for business and pleasure.
There has been _____ in the overseas travel market.

15. Compared with five years ago, more people are shopping in out-of-town malls than in local stores.
There has been an _____ in the number of people shopping in out-of-town malls.

16. Unless your work visibly improves, we will have to recommend a transfer to another department.
We need to see some _____ in your work, or we will recommend a departmental transfer.

17. Young Americans want to travel, meet new people and see more of the world than their parents and grandparents did.
Young Americans want to _____ their horizons.

18. Over the next two months, we plan to make our office computers faster and more efficient.
Over the next two months, we plan to _____ our office computers.

19. We are trying to make the accounting system simpler and more efficient.
We are trying to _____ the accounting system.

20. Making the company smaller by making a lot of staff members redundant has made it much more profitable than it was before.
_____ the company has made it much more profitable than it was before.

21. Standards of service have gone down recently, and as a result we have lost a lot of customers.
Standards of service have _____ recently, and as a result we have lost a lot of customers.

22. Property prices have gone up, then gone down, then gone up again this year.
Property prices have _____ this year.

23. We have made small changes to the rules for applying for instant credit.
We have _____ the rules for applying for instant credit.

24. The company is planning to change its marketing division to make it more effective.
The company is planning to _____ its marketing division.

Also see *Changes 2* on page 3.

For reference see *Easier English Intermediate Dictionary* (0-7475-6989-4).

Changes 2

The box below contains 27 words used to describe change in different situations. These are all verbs, and they can be found by reading from left to right and from right to left, starting in the top-left corner and following the direction of the arrows. Separate these words, then use some of them to complete sentences 1 – 10 below. In some cases you will need to change the form of the verb (for example, by putting it into its past simple or past participle form).

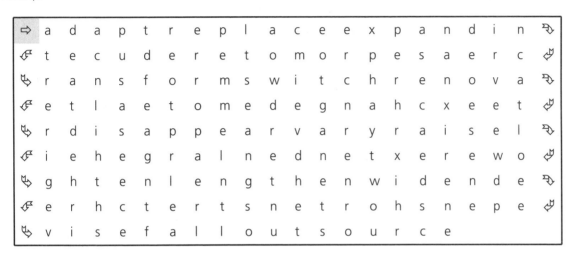

1. The company cannot refund customers' money, and goods can only be _____ on production of a receipt or other proof of purchase.

2. We have made radical changes to the working regulations, and employees are expected to _____ to these over the next few weeks.

3. Our customer call center used to be in Wichita, but last year we _____ it to India, where costs are much lower.

4. The new director has completely _____ the company, from a small local enterprise to a major international concern.

5. The hotel is currently being _____, but will remain open while building work is carried out.

6. Production has been _____ from our Boston site to a new industrial center outside of Portland.

7. Our new memory cards _____ in price, from $35 for a 64Mb card up to $125 for a 2Gb card.

8. The Internet clothing company *Pants-2-U.com* has _____ its range to include jewelry and watches.

9. After the sales manager lost the company almost $20,000 in a bad deal, the director had no choice but to _____ him to sales assistant.

10. Air fares will be _____ on July 21: domestic flights will go down by 10%, but international flights will go up by 22%.

Also see *Changes 1* on pages 1 and 2.

For reference see *Easier English Intermediate Dictionary* (0-7475-6989-4).

Comparing and contrasting

Complete these sentences with the most appropriate word or expression in **bold**. In one case, all three options are possible.

1. The **contrast / compare / comparison** in working conditions between our Denver department and our department in Chicago is very noticeable, and employees are now demanding equality in this area.

2. The two companies **differentiate / differ / different** considerably from each other: one sells to the wholesale market, and one sells directly to retailers.

3. It is often difficult to **differentiate / differ / contrast** between employees who are off work because they are genuinely ill, and those who are just enjoying a day at home.

4. Our new software program shares some common **characters / characterizes / characteristics** with those that are already on the market.

5. There's a clear **distinguish / distinctive / distinction** between starting your own company, and taking over one that already exists.

6. **Compared / Compare / Comparing** with 15 years ago, home PCs are cheaper, faster and have a much bigger memory.

7. The two products are different in every way: there's absolutely no **compare / comparison / contrast** between them.

8. Our latest mobile phones **similar to / alike / resemble** those of our main competitor, except that they have more features and are more reliable.

9. There are several **similarities / similarly / similar to** between our new photocopier and our old one: these include an advanced color facility and a multi-task option.

10. Serious computer hackers can access your personal files and destroy or alter them. **Exactly / In the same way / Just as**, they can gain access to your Internet banking facility and steal your money.

11. The quality of our products is excellent. **Likewise / Alike / Likeness**, the price.

12. The TOEFL® exam covers a variety of general English tasks. **In contrast to / Although / By way of contrast**, the TOEIC® focuses more on business and professional issues.

13. The company has not performed very well during the last quarter. **Nevertheless / Even so / However**, it has still managed to turn a profit and retain most of its clients.

14. There currently seems to be a large **discrepancy / discrimination / differential** between the number of people employed in service industries, and those employed in the primary sector.

15. Our new contract states that both parties must give 6 months' notice of termination, **unlike / whereas / whereby** our old contract had an immediate 'get-out' clause.

For reference see *Easier English Intermediate Dictionary* (0-7475-6989-4).

Computers and information technology

Read the text below, in which someone is talking about their computer. Unfortunately, they have used rather 'un-technical' language. Replace the words and expressions in **bold** with something more appropriate from the box.

CD drive   components   CPU (Central Processing Unit)   desktop   DTP (desktop publishing)
flash-drive   hard disk   hard drive   keyboard   laptop   load   memory   monitor
mouse   printer   scanner   software   spreadsheet   USB port   word processing

---

This is my new (1) **computer that sits on top of a table or desk** (I've also got a (2) **small computer which can be carried or placed on your knees**). As you can see, there are six main (3) **parts** to it. The first is the (4) **part of the computer that runs it and controls what it does**, and this is the most important bit. It carries the (5) **part that stores and controls the flow of information**, including the (6) **round thing that is used for storing information**. Mine has a particularly high (7) **capacity for storing information**, which means that it's much faster than most. It came with its own (8) **computer programs** package (including (9) **writing, checking and changing texts**, (10) **calculating in columns of figures**, and (11) **producing texts and pictures for magazines** packages). You can also (12) **put in** other programs using the (13) **sliding tray for carrying round, plastic, information-holding things**, or the (14) **hole for connecting computer parts to one another** (into which you can put a (15) **small plastic and metal stick which can hold a lot of information**). The other five parts of the computer are the (16) **screen that lets you see what your computer is doing**, the (17) **flat thing with the letters and numbers on it that let you control the computer**, the (18) **machine that lets you make copies of the documents that you create on your computer**, the (19) **device for making color copies of photographs and other documents which you can put onto your computer**, and last but not least, the (20) **device that you hold in your hand and move across your desk to control the cursor**.

Instructions as above

---

access   attachment   bookmark   browser   chatrooms   crashing   delete
download   email   homepage   Internet   keywords   links   log on   log out
online   pop-up   provider   search engine   spam   upgrade   virus   website

---

Now, in my opinion, the best thing about modern information technology is the (1) **network that links millions of computers from around the world**. Once you've got yourself a / an (2) **company that allows you** (3) **entry**, and a (4) **program that finds information** you can start using this. It's especially useful if you want to get information about something, go shopping or (5) **transfer** information, games, music, etc., onto your own computer. You can even 'talk' to other computer users in (6) **special places where you can leave messages and get instant replies**. Most companies have their own (7) **special computer pages**

For reference see *Easier English Intermediate Dictionary* (0-7475-6989-4).

which you can look at. Let me (8) **turn the computer on, enter my code and access the computer system**, and I'll show you ours. OK, here we go. Oh no, another (9) **advertisement that suddenly appears on the computer screen**. How annoying. Let me just remove it. That's better.

Now, I can never remember the exact address of our company, so first of all I'll type it into the (10) **program that helps you find the information you want**. OK, A & C Black Publishing. The computer identifies the (11) **most important or main words** and then gives me (12) **connections** to a list of possible sites. This one looks right: www.acblack.com. I'll click on that. Bingo! Here's our (13) **front page**. You can use this to find the different books that we publish, and if you want you can even buy them (14) **through the computer**. Hmm, this book looks good: Check Your English Vocabulary for TOEIC®. Now, before I (15) **exit this site**, I'll just (16) **add it to my list of favorites** so that I can find it more quickly next time.

Perhaps the most important thing, however, is (17) **a special electronic letter-sending facility**, which allows you to communicate with people around the world in an instant. Let me quickly check mine. Oh dear, nothing very interesting. Mainly a load of (18) **unwanted advertising**. I'll just (19) **remove** it: I don't particularly want to rent a vacation home in Mexico, have my future read by one of America's top astrologers or buy a phone that lets you smell the person you're talking to. There's something here from my sister with a / an (20) **document or file that has been sent with it**. You have to be careful with these: sometimes they contain a (21) **hidden routine placed in the program that destroys or corrupts files**. If you open it, it can do all sorts of horrible things to your computer. I had one last week that kept (22) **shutting down** my computer. I do have a protection package, but it's a bit out of date: I really ought to (23) **bring it up to date**.

The exercises above contain just a few of the words and expressions related to computers and IT. Many more enter our vocabulary each year. How many others do you know?

For reference see *Easier English Intermediate Dictionary* (0-7475-6989-4).

Condition and requirement

Rearrange the letters in **bold** to make words and expressions related to condition and requirement. The first one has been done as an example.

1. **sa nlgo sa** customers continue to demand the BD17 model mobile, Telelink will continue to produce it. If demand falls, the line will be discontinued.
   (Answer = As long as)

2. **seusln** we receive your payment within ten days, we will have to start charging you interest.

3. We will continue to offer you interest-free credit **no incotnido atth** you maintain regular repayments to your account. The minimum monthly repayment is $250.

4. Everyone will get a pay rise **vogrnipid ttha** we meet our sales targets.

5. The main **retncopiinod** for increased consumer spending is a stable economy with low inflation and low interest rates. Without these, people will save rather than spend.

6. (Notice on a fire alarm): **ni eacs fo** fire, break class.

7. **ni het nvete fo** a delay, all passengers will receive a voucher for a light meal at the airport.

8. We agreed to sign the contract, the only **aputonstili** being that it would run for at least five years.

9. The management has **nidncoalitoun** trust in its employees: it knows they will do their best at all times, even if things get difficult.

10. **sumsagin hatt** the flight is on time, we will meet you at LaGuardia airport at ten o'clock.

11. We will proceed with the delivery of spare parts **no teh autonmsspi hatt** your order has remained unchanged.

12. Being able to drive is one of the **quereesisitpr** of the job: if you cannot drive, you will not be considered for the post.

13. Before you accept a job, it is important that you agree with the **remst** and **ioctnsodin** set out in the contract.

14. It is a **nmreiretque** of the company that employees have a medical at least once a year.

15. If you have a query, telephone us at the number above. **niifagl ttha**, send us an email.

16. We need to involve at least 20 people on this project, **ehewotris** it can't go ahead.

For reference see *Easier English Intermediate Dictionary* (0-7475-6989-4).

Confusing words

The sentences below are all missing one word. Four possible answers follow each sentence. Choose the best answer in each case. Note that each set of answers includes some words that are often confused with one another, either because: (a) they are related to the same topic, but have a different meaning; (b) they look similar but have a different meaning; (c) they are English words which have a similar-looking word in another language but which have a different meaning (we call these words *false friends*).

1. Try to make your report as _____ as possible: only give us the facts, and not your opinions.
    (a) **subjective**   (b) **objectionable**   (c) **subjected**   (d) **objective**

2. Environmental inspectors regularly _____ our kitchens and other food preparation areas to make sure they conform to regulations.
    (a) **inspect**   (b) **control**   (c) **study**   (d) **analyze**

3. _____ workers are often rewarded with higher salaries and other benefits.
    (a) **conscious**   (b) **conscientious**   (c) **conscience**   (d) **consciousness**

4. Airlines are already increasing their prices on the _____ that fuel prices are going to rise.
    (a) **consumption**   (b) **destruction**   (c) **assumption**   (d) **presumption**

5. The fire caused a lot of _____ to the building and factory machinery.
    (a) **damage**   (b) **harm**   (c) **injury**   (d) **wound**

6. Government subsidies helped to _____ many companies being forced to close down.
    (a) **prevent**   (b) **preventive**   (c) **avoidance**   (d) **avoid**

7. The manager made it clear that he intended to _____ down some new rules to enforce workplace discipline.
    (a) **lying**   (b) **lie**   (c) **laying**   (d) **lay**

8. Cuts in advertising will have a serious _____ on sales.
    (a) **effective**   (b) **effect**   (c) **affect**   (d) **affection**

9. If you want to take photographs, you will need to apply for a _____.
    (a) **permit**   (b) **permission**   (c) **permissible**   (d) **permitting**

10. At the meeting, the manager talked _____ about the need for better attendance and punctuality.
    (a) **briefly**   (b) **briefing**   (c) **shortly**   (d) **shorts**

11. The office will be closed _____ it is being decorated.
    (a) **during**   (b) **while**   (c) **for**   (d) **throughout**

12. Can you _____ me on the best course of action to take?
    (a) **advisory**   (b) **advisable**   (c) **advice**   (d) **advise**

13. Economic _____ slowly stagnated as the recession became worse.
    (a) **active**   (b) **action**   (c) **activity**   (d) **activist**

14. _____ their regular daytime job, many people do extra work in the evening.
    (a) **by**   (b) **beside**   (c) **between**   (d) **besides**

15. The computer system crashed on Monday, then again on Wednesday and finally today. These

For reference see *Easier English Intermediate Dictionary* (0-7475-6989-4).

_____ breakdowns are wasting us time and costing us a lot of money.
(a) **continuing** (b) **continuous** (c) **continuation** (d) **continual**

16. She was very _____ of our efforts to help.
(a) **appreciable** (b) **appreciative** (c) **appreciating** (d) **appreciate**

17. The manager said he believed we would win the contract, but I knew that we didn't really stand a / an _____.
(a) **possibility** (b) **probability** (c) **chance** (d) **opportunity**

18. The proposals he put forward were excellent. _____, it quickly became apparent that they would work when put into practice.
(a) **Moreover** (b) **However** (c) **Nevertheless** (d) **Although**

19. We need to remain _____ to the needs of our customers, and react accordingly.
(a) **sensible** (b) **sensitive** (c) **sensitivity** (d) **sensibility**

20. A _____ amount of working hours are lost every year because of illness and absenteeism.
(a) **considerate** (b) **considerable** (c) **consistent** (d) **convenient**

21. The new salesman refused to wear a tie on _____.
(a) **principle** (b) **principality** (c) **principal** (d) **principally**

22. Nobody raised any _____ when we insisted on opening an hour earlier.
(a) **criticism** (b) **complaints** (c) **protests** (d) **objections**

23. The museum contains several _____ works of Renaissance art, including two paintings by Raphael, one by Dürer, one by Titian, and an early sketch by Tintoretto.
(a) **worthless** (b) **valueless** (c) **priceless** (d) **useless**

24. Despite the recent economic recovery, many people are still looking for _____.
(a) **work** (b) **job** (c) **profession** (d) **career**

25. The Avicenna Partnership is a _____ company with a long and successful sales history.
(a) **respectable** (b) **respectful** (c) **respecting** (d) **respective**

26. Because of increased operating costs, we have been forced to _____ our prices.
(a) **rise** (b) **raze** (c) **raise** (d) **arise**

27. The bank has said it will be happy to _____ us the money provided we have suitable collateral.
(a) **lend** (b) **borrow** (c) **lease** (d) **rent**

28. When we leave the office tonight, _____ me to turn everything off and lock up properly.
(a) **remembrance** (b) **reminisce** (c) **remember** (d) **remind**

29. Because of the current _____ situation, we have been forced to close down several of our city center outlets.
(a) **economical** (b) **economic** (c) **economize** (d) **economics**

30. Shortly before you hold a meeting, it is a good idea to send everyone in the office a _____ outlining the main points to be discussed.
(a) **notify** (b) **notice** (c) **note** (d) **notification**

For reference see *Easier English Intermediate Dictionary* (0-7475-6989-4).

Continuing, repeating and starting again

Exercise 1: The sentences below all contain a word or expression in bold referring to *continuing something*, *repeating something*, or *starting something again*. In some of the sentences, the word has been used correctly. In others, the wrong word has been used.

Identify which sentences are correct and which are wrong. Replace the words in the wrong sentences with a correct word. You will find these words in the other wrong sentences.

1.   Despite **repeated** warnings, you have failed to show any improvement in your work or your attitude.

2.   The production line has been temporarily shut down following a report from the Health and Safety officer, but we hope to **ongoing** production as soon as possible.

3.   The meeting will break for lunch at half past twelve, and **restart** at two.

4.   I think that we have talked enough about planning permission for the new office. I would like to **reopen** to the previous subject of overdue payments, if that's all right?

5.   We like to **continuous** good relations with our customers, and take any complaints very seriously indeed.

6.   The computer crashed on Monday, then again on Wednesday and once more on Friday. If it gives us **persevere** problems, I suggest we get a new one.

7.   A regular, repeated tone means that the person you are trying to call is already on the phone, but a / an **maintain** tone means that the number you are trying to call is not available.

8.   We are worried that work on the new warehouse will **progress** too slowly unless we offer the contractors more incentives.

9.   We understand that you are supposed to retire next month, but we would be delighted if you would **carry on** working for us after that on a part-time basis.

10. The economic climate is very bad at the moment, and we are losing over $10,000 a month as a result, but I suggest we **steady** and hope that recovery comes soon.

11. Unfortunately, the latest company report will **persist** the rumor that we are going to close down some departments.

12. The managing director called, and says he wants us to **press on** with the proposed changes to the distribution scheme despite opposition from the marketing department.

13. The hotel will be closed for renovations between October 15 and November 20, but will **revert** in time for the Thanksgiving holiday.

14. The Directors have said they are delighted with the commitment you have shown the company this year, and hope that you will be able to **perpetuate** the good work.

15. If you **continual** in coming late and taking unauthorized breaks, we will have no option but to dismiss you from your post.

10

For reference see *Easier English Intermediate Dictionary* (0-7475-6989-4).

16. Staff absenteeism is a / an **keep up** problem which we need to resolve as soon as possible.

17. The **constant** noise from the highway outside the office makes it very difficult to concentrate.

18. As long as the negotiations continue to **proceed** well, we hope to sign the contract by the end of the month.

19. Unemployment figures have fallen by about 2% every year for the last ten years. It is hoped that this **resume** decrease will continue.

20. If the government agrees to **pursue** its current policy of reducing taxation, we can afford to invest more in developing our technology.

Exercise 2: Complete these sentences using the most appropriate word or expression from Exercise 1. In some cases you will need to change the form of the word (for example, from an adjective to an adverb), and in some cases more than one option is possible.

1. We have asked them _____ to send us the invoice, but they have ignored us every time.

2. The air conditioning is _____ breaking down, usually when it's really hot.

3. Sales figures have been dropping by about 3% a month. If this problem _____, we will have to start making staff cutbacks.

4. Rail services between Albion Creek and Elgin City have been suspended while the track is repaired, but will _____ early next week.

5. Learning a language isn't easy. You need to _____ if you want to make any real progress.

6. One of the most important things you should do in this line of work is _____ a sense of humor, especially when things go wrong.

7. The work on the new airport isn't _____ fast enough, and won't be ready in time for the beginning of the tourist season.

8. The presentation ended early because of _____ interruptions from the audience.

9. Staff development workshops help our team to develop new and more effective ways of working, but eventually many of them _____ to their old ways.

10. Everyone is delighted with the quality of service you provide. _____ it _____!

For reference see *Easier English Intermediate Dictionary* (0-7475-6989-4).

Contracts

Look at paragraphs 1 – 6 in the boxes, and answer the questions that follow them.

1.

> This contract is <u>binding</u>, and we expect all the <u>parts</u> involved (both clients and suppliers) to <u>abide by</u> the <u>terms and conditions</u> stated in sections 3a – 37g on pages 1 – 17.

1. One of the <u>underlined</u> words / expressions in the above sentence is wrong. Identify and correct it.
2. True or false: A contract which is *binding* is flexible and can be changed at any time.
3. Which of these words / expressions could replace *abide by*?:
   (A) choose   (B) agree with   (C) obey   (D) change

2.

> On <u>terminator</u> of this contract, the company will be <u>obliged</u> to return any unused materials to the supplier within 28 days, unless <u>provision</u> has been made for a temporary extension. If any of the rules of the contract are <u>broken</u>, all materials must be returned immediately.

1. One of the <u>underlined</u> words / expressions in the above sentence is wrong. Identify and correct it.
2. True or false: *Provision* has a similar meaning to *arrangement*.
3. Rearrange these letters to make two words which have a similar meaning to *obliged*:
   degabtlio   edequrir

3.

> The contract was originally <u>verbal</u>, but we've finally managed to get the company to give us something on paper. They say that this contract is <u>un-negotiable</u>, but maybe we can persuade them to <u>amend</u> some of the details before we sign <u>on the dotted line</u>.

1. One of the <u>underlined</u> words / expressions in the above paragraph is wrong. Identify and correct it.
2. True or false: The speaker thinks that it might be possible for small changes to be made to the contract before she signs it.
3. Rearrange the letters in **bold** to make four words which have the same meaning as *verbal* in this situation
   rola   kosnep   plidemi   etodnurdso

12

For reference see *Easier English Intermediate Dictionary* (0-7475-6989-4).

4.

> Swillpot Airline Catering Ltd were <u>sued</u> by Pan-Globe Airways when they were found to be <u>in beach of</u> their contract, specifically that they had failed to <u>comply with</u> <u>clause</u> 27B, which stated that their food should be "fit for human consumption."

1.   One of the <u>underlined</u> words / expressions in the above sentence is wrong. Identify and correct it.
2.   Find a word or expression in paragraphs 1 – 3 above which has a similar meaning to *comply with* in paragraph 4.
3.   True or false: Pan-Globe Airways are unhappy with Swillpot Airline Catering because they have breached *all* of their contractual terms.

5.

> Withers Interiors Ltd have entered into an <u>agreement</u> with Sophos Construction to act as sole providers of quality interior fittings <u>commencing</u> 15 August this year. This is to run for 18 months, with a 3 month <u>period of notification</u> in the event of <u>cancellation</u> by either side.

1.   One of the <u>underlined</u> words / expressions in the above sentence is wrong. Identify and correct it.
2.   Which word in the paragraph is the closest in meaning to the noun *contract*?
3.   True or false: If either Withers Interiors Ltd or Sophos Construction want to end the contract, they must tell the other company 3 months before they do it.

6.

> This contract recognizes the <u>anointment</u> of Mr. Alan Wiley as non-executive Director to the board of AKL Publishing following the company's <u>amalgamation</u> with Berryhill Books. While Mr. Wiley may continue to buy stocks in the company, he may not acquire a <u>controlling interest</u>, and he may have no professional dealings with any <u>third parties</u> during this period.

1.   One of the <u>underlined</u> words / expressions in the above sentence is wrong. Identify and correct it.
2.   True or false: AKL Publishing recently separated from Berryhill Books.
3.   Mr. Wiley can buy as many shares as he likes in the company.
4.   In addition to sitting on the board of AKL Publishing, how many other companies can Mr. Wiley work for?

For reference see *Easier English Intermediate Dictionary* (0-7475-6989-4).

Different situations

Look at paragraphs 1 – 10, and answer the question that follows each one.

1.

If it is formal, it should begin with a polite salutation. If you don't know the recipient's name, call them *Sir* or *Madam*, but if you know their name, always use it (beginning with *Mr.* for men and *Ms.* for women). It should be brief, clear and to the point. End with *Yours sincerely* if you know the recipient's name, or *Yours faithfully* if you don't. Some people end theirs with *Yours truly*. Only use *Best wishes* at the end if it is informal.

■ *What is the speaker talking about?*

2.

Mr. Jenkins: What's the schedule for today?
Ms. Ranscombe: Well, after everyone has arrived and registered, there will be coffee in the reception area. This will give everyone a chance to meet their fellow delegates and do some networking. This will be followed by a plenary session in the main hall: I believe the speaker will be giving a presentation on new marketing trends. After a break at 11 o'clock there will be different seminars for areas of special interest. The afternoon will consist of a series of workshops, and then there will be an evening reception and dinner for all the participants.

■ *Where are Mr. Jenkins and Ms. Ranscombe?*

3.

Ms. Akkabar: Hello, Mr. Andrews. What can I do for you today?
Mr. Andrews: I originally just wanted a checkup, but two days ago I lost a filling, and I think one of my crowns is coming loose. I guess that will be expensive to fix.
Ms. Akkabar: Well, it might be, but we have various payment options that might spread the cost. Take a seat and I'll have a look. Hmm. Your gums look a bit sore. How often do you brush and floss?
Mr. Andrews: About five times a day!

■ *What is Ms. Akkabar's job?*

4.

Our company is committed to helping employees learn more about their jobs and develop their skills, so we run regular sessions to facilitate this. These are usually in the form of seminars and workshops, and cover a wide range of subjects, including leadership skills, problem solving, decision-making, negotiation skills and interpersonal development. Our employees can then revise and practice these skills through our online program which is run on the company intranet.

■ *True or false: The speaker thinks that his employees don't work hard enough.*

5.

Is that Amanda Mellors? Oh, well, could you put me through then? You can't get through? Oh, her line is engaged. I see. No, I can't hang on, I'm afraid. Could you give me her extension? It's confidential, is it? Well, could you ask her to get back to me later? Hello? HELLO? I don't believe it, I've been cut off.

■ *What is the speaker doing?*

For reference see *Easier English Intermediate Dictionary* (0-7475-6989-4).

6.

Each employee has at least one of these a year. Each session lasts about 45 minutes, and we ask them various questions. For example, we ask them if they think the work they are doing meets the correct standards and whether or not they have met the objectives we have set for them. We also like to know if they are happy with the way their career is progressing, if they would like to do something more challenging, and also if they receive sufficient encouragement, praise and motivation from their managers.

■ *Rearrange the letters in bold to make words: The speaker is talking about his company's* **fatfs spapialar** *program.*

7.

My boss is abrasive, bigoted, conceited, confrontational, critical, insensitive, intolerant and obstinate.

■ *Does the speaker have a good boss or a bad one?*

8.

Ms. Collins: You will be expected to oversee the work of the production department, agree product specifications with sales departments and time schedules with the stock control department, ensure the product is manufactured according to agreed specifications, inspect the quality of the finished product, produce sales reports for the head office, visit and negotiate with suppliers on base material prices and deal with everyday problems as they arise.
Mr. Sheppard: Anything else?
Ms. Collins: Yes. Make my coffee. Two sugars and plenty of cream, please.

■ *What is Ms. Collins explaining to Mr. Sheppard?*

9.

Ms. Colley: What's your diagnosis? Is it serious?
Mr. Sagala: Oh no. You have a throat infection, but it's fairly minor and nothing to worry about.
Ms. Colley: Can you treat it?
Mr. Sagala: Oh yes, I'll give you a prescription for antibiotics. They should cure it. But make an appointment to come back and see me in a week. It's contagious, so I suggest you take a few days off work. I'll write you a sick note.

■ *How does Mr. Sagala make his living?*

10.

Mr. Samson: This says we owe them $180, but the order was only for $131.
Ms. Grant: Yes, but that price was exclusive of tax.
Mr. Samson: I know, but even with tax it should only come to $165.
Ms. Grant: That's true. Oh, hang on, look what it says at the bottom. Package and delivery: $15.
Mr. Samson: Oh, right. Well, I guess we had better pay them. Who do we make the remittance payable to?
Ms. Grant: Oh, we don't need to send them anything. The payment will be automatically deducted from our account at the end of the month. Unfortunately, what this doesn't show us is the import duty we will have to pay. I guess we can expect to get a bill from Customs soon.

■ *What are Mr. Samson and Ms. Grant looking at?*

Look at the situations again, and highlight the key words and expressions that helped you to identify what each one is about.

For reference see *Easier English Intermediate Dictionary* (0-7475-6989-4).

Earnings, rewards and benefits

Complete the first part of each word in **bold** in sentences 1 – 32 with the second part in the box.

-an	-ance	-ance	-ans	-ary	-ated	-ation	-ay	-ble	-count	-ction	-dancy
-den	-dex	-diture	-ement	-ensurate	-eration	-et	-faction	-fit	-ge		
-hting	-imum	-ise	-ission	-kage	-ked	-lement	-me	-nus	-ock	-ome	
-ormance	-oss	-ring	-roll	-shake	-sion	-slip	-te	-time	-tions	-tive	-ve

1. A *wage* is money that is normally paid to an employee on a weekly basis, and a **sal____** is money that is usually paid to an employee on a monthly basis.

2. **Remun____** is the formal word for money that an employee receives for doing his / her job.

3. When we work for more than the normal working time, we say that we work (and therefore earn) **over____**.

4. An automatic and regular increase in pay is called an **incr____**.

5. Money that is removed from our earnings to pay for tax, national insurance, etc., is called a **dedu____**.

6. The **min____ wa____** is the lowest hourly wage which a company can legally pay its employees.

7. Time for which work is paid at twice the normal rate (for example, on national holidays) is called **dou____ ti____**.

8. A **pen____ pl____** helps people to save money for when they retire from work.

9. When you want more money for the work you do, you might ask your boss for a **ra____**.

10. If an employee needs some of his / her wages paid before the usual pay day, he / she might ask for an **adv____**.

11. A **pay____** shows an employee how much pay he / she has received, and how much has been removed for tax, insurance, etc.

12. An extra payment made in addition to a normal payment (usually received by sales people for selling more than their quota) is called a **bo____**.

13. A **pay____** is the list a company keeps that shows all the people employed and paid by that company.

14. A rewards **pac____** is the money and other benefits offered with a job.

15. A **weig____** is an additional amount of money paid to an employee to compensate him / her for living in an expensive area.

16. By law, American companies have to give their employees the right to take paid vacations: this is known as **lea____ entit____**.

For reference see *Easier English Intermediate Dictionary* (0-7475-6989-4).

17. **Inc____** is another word for the money that people receive for working. The money that they spend is known as **expen____**.

18. For some people, the money that they earn for doing a job is less important than job **satis____** (the pleasure they get from doing their job).

19. A sales person usually earns a percentage of the sales value of the product or service he / she sells: this is called a **comm____** .

20. Some companies offer their employees **st____ op____**, which means that the employees can buy stocks at a price lower than the normal price.

21. Some companies have **incen____ pl____**, where they offer their employees extra rewards and benefits for good attendance, increased productivity, etc.

22. The amount of money an employee receives each hour, day, week, etc., is known as an hourly / daily / weekly **ra____**.

23. If an employee loses his / her job because the company doesn't need or can't afford to keep him / her, they might receive **redun____ p____**.

24. Some companies offer their employees a **dis____** on the product and services they sell, which means that the employee can buy them for less than the usual price.

25. If an employee takes a job in another town or city which is a long way from his / her original home and place of work, he / she might be offered a **reloc____ allow____**.

26. Some companies have a policy of **pro____ sha____**, where some or all of the money that they make is given to their employees.

27. **Gr____** is an adjective used to describe an employee's earnings *before* tax, national insurance, etc., have been removed.

28. **N____** is an adjective used to describe an employee's earnings *after* tax, national insurance, etc., have been removed.

29. When the money that an employee receives rises automatically by the percentage increase in the cost of living, we say that it is **in____-lin____**.

30. If the amount of money an employee receives depends on how well he / she does his / her job, we say that it is **perf____-rel____**.

31. When the money that an employee earns is based on age, experience, qualifications, position in the company, etc., we say that it is **comm____**.

32. When an employee leaves his / her job after a long period with the company, he / she might be offered a large amount of money known as a **gol____ hand____**.

For reference see *Easier English Intermediate Dictionary* (0-7475-6989-4).

Entertainment, art, sports and the media

Complete paragraphs A – H with words from the box below each one and decide what the speaker is talking about in each case. In some cases, more than one answer may be possible.

(A)

After a very successful year in which they had the country's highest (1)_____, their (2)_____ has dropped recently. This has come as a major surprise, as their (3)_____ of major national and world (4)_____ is excellent, their (5)_____ and (6)_____ are well-(7)_____, and they approach (8)_____ affairs in a way that is (9)_____, but (10)_____ and interesting. Did you know that the (11)_____ and several (12)_____ recently won a National (13)_____ Club award?

articles	circulation	coverage	current	editor	events	features	journalists	lively
		objective	Press	readership	researched			

(B)

There was clearly a (1)_____ problem in the (2)_____. You could see the (3)_____, but you couldn't hear her. However, you could hear the (4)_____, who obviously didn't realise that even though he was (5)_____ he was still (6)_____, and was going out (7)_____ across the entire (8)_____! You wouldn't have believed the language he was using: I bet there were a few (9)_____ from viewers to the (10)_____ standards committee after that! It was so funny that I was really disappointed when they cut to a commercial (11)_____.

anchor	break	broadcasting	complaints	live	network	off-screen
	on air	reporter	studio	technical		

(C)

This is one of the most famous (1)_____ by the American (2)_____ Ernest Hemingway, and one for which he won the Nobel prize for (3)_____. What I like about it is the simple (4)_____, and the fact that the main (5)_____ is a simple, everyday man fighting the forces of nature. It is (6)_____ in Cuba, and the (7)_____ takes place mainly at sea. It's semi-(8)_____, as the man really existed. I would (9)_____ it very much. It has recently been re-(10)_____ in an (11)_____ of the man's greatest works: I suggest you pick up a (12)_____ as soon as you can.

action	anthology	writer	biographical	character	copy	issued
	literature	plot	recommend	set	works	

(D)

I'm not particularly keen on the (1)_____'s style, but his latest offering is excellent and is bound to be a (2)_____ success. I wouldn't even be surprised if it picked up an Academy (3)_____ or two (or three or four). Apart from the (4)_____, who give an amazing (5)_____, the special (6)_____ are excellent, the (7)_____ is stunning, the (8)_____ is very impressive, and there is a lively (9)_____. When it finished, even cynical (10)_____ such as myself were applauding. You should go and see it as soon as it is on general (11)_____.

actors	Award	box-office	cinematography	critics	director	effects
	performance	release	scenery	soundtrack		

For reference see *Easier English Intermediate Dictionary* (0-7475-6989-4).

(E)

This was the (1)_____ night, and from what I could see, many in the (2)_____ were probably hoping it would be the last: by the time the (3)_____ had opened and the (4)_____ had come up on the (5)_____ for the second (6)_____ of the (7)_____, the (8)_____ was half empty. The (9)_____ clearly hadn't (10)_____ enough and kept forgetting their (11)_____, the (12)_____ was as wooden as a tree, and the (13)_____ looked like it had been put together by a five-year-old. The (14)_____ were probably in tears at the money they would be losing, and if the (15)_____ moved to Mars, I doubt anyone would be sorry.

audience	auditorium	backers	cast	curtain	dialog	half	lights	lines
opening	performance	rehearsed	scenery	scriptwriter	stage			

(F)

There are over 30 (1)_____ holding a total of over 50,000 (2)_____, of which about 3000 come from (3)_____ Egypt, and which were (4)_____ from a private (5)_____ in the 1950s. There is also an excellent section on modern (6)_____, which has a permanent (7)_____ of landscapes, (8)_____, sculptures and still lifes by some of the 20th century's most (9)_____ and significant (10)_____. There are regular temporary (11)_____ as well. (12)_____ is free for everyone, although visitors are encouraged to make a voluntary (13)_____ of $5 to help pay for the upkeep.

accomplished	acquired	admission	ancient	art	artists	collection
collector	contribution	exhibitions	exhibits	galleries	portraits	

(G)

I am not particularly keen on live (1)_____, and I usually avoid heavy-metal rock (2)_____ like *The Würst*, but this is different. From the opening (3)_____ on the first (4)_____, to the last cheers of the (5)_____ as they worship their leather- clad heroes, you are there with the (6)_____ as they go through their (7)_____ of (8)_____. The sound is crystal-clear throughout, there are some interesting (9)_____ on the usual (10)_____ versions, and some witty and (11)_____ comments to the (12)_____ from lead (13)_____ and guitarist Oswald Batmüncher. If you like this, you should also check out their latest (14)_____ *The Very Best of The Würst*, which contains 16 of their most famous numbers from the last 10 years.

astute	band	compilation	crowd	fans	groups	hits	note
recordings	repertoire	singer	studio	track	variations		

(H)

The (1)_____ in the (2)_____ cheered and clapped as the (3)_____ came onto the (4)_____. Who would (5)_____ the event? Would the Denver Deadbeats (6)_____ again? Or would it be the Washington Wasters' time to (7)_____ their deadliest (8)_____ at last? The (9)_____ shook hands, the (10)_____ tossed a coin, and it was game on! The (11)_____ urged their (12)_____ on with their well-practiced routine, the (13)_____ sang and chanted slogans, and the (14)_____ shouted advice and (15)_____ from the sidelines. The final (16)_____: a (17)_____ at 4 goals each.

beat	captains	cheerleaders	coaches	draw	encouragement
opponents	pitch	players	referee	score	spectators	stadium
supporters	teams	triumph	win		

19

For reference see *Easier English Intermediate Dictionary* (0-7475-6989-4).

Food and eating out

Test your knowledge with this vocabulary quiz.

1. Look at this formal notice printed at the bottom of a menu. Replace the formal words and expressions in **bold** with less formal words. (1 point each. Total: 6 points)
"*Patrons* are *requested* to *refrain from* smoking in the *dining area*. If they *wish* to smoke, they should *retire* to the bar."
(a) _____ are (b) _____ (c) _____ to smoke in the (d) _____. If they (e) _____ to smoke, they should (f) _____ to the bar.

2. This extract from an article on healthy eating contains 2 factual mistakes. Can you identify them (2 points) and correct them (2 points)? (Total: 4 points)
Wholesome food should always be rich in vitamins and minerals, have a minimum amount of sugar and salt, be free from preservatives and other artificial ingredients, and be high in cholesterol. The best way of preparing meat and vegetables is to fry them, as this helps them to retain all their goodness.

3. Find words or expressions in the above extract that are closest in meaning to:
(a) *the part or parts of a food that are healthy for you*   (b) *the different things that are needed to make a meal*   (c) *containing a lot of something* (2 possible answers)   (d) *very small*   (e) *keep*
(f) *healthy*   (g) *cooking*   (h) *lacking / not having*   (i) *not real / not genuine*   (j) *method*
(1 point each. Total: 10 points)

4. Rearrange the letters in **bold** to make words (1 point each. Total: 3 points):
*A person who doesn't eat meat is called a / an **tagaenevri**. A person who doesn't eat any products from or produced by animals (including milk, eggs, cheese, honey, etc.) is called a / an **ganev**. A person who doesn't drink alcohol is called a / an **realtottee**.*

5. Complete these sentences with an appropriate preposition or particle (1 point for each preposition / particle or combination. Total: 8 points):
(a) *I can't eat nuts because I'm allergic _____ them.*
(b) *He's not keen _____ Asian food in general, but he is very fond _____ Japanese food, especially sushi .*
(c) *My doctor has advised me to cut _____ _____ my salt intake, and cut _____ meat from my diet altogether.*
(d) *I wish I could give _____ eating candy, but I like it too much!*
(e) *This meat smells really bad. I think it's gone _____.*
(f) *What's _____ lunch? And what are we going to drink _____ it?*

6. This extract from an article on food contains <u>five</u> wrong words. Can you find them and correct them? (1 point each. Total: 5 points)
More consumers these days are interested in where their food comes from. As a result, there is now much more demand for things like free ranger eggs, and organism fruit, vegetables and meat. People are also more concerned about artificial additions and colorings in their food, and of course everyone is worried about the potential dangers of genetically modification (GM) food. As a result, fat food outlets are beginning to lose customers.

7. Rearrange the letters in **bold** to make words and expressions (1 point each. Total: 14 points)
*I really would not **meordcenm** the new restaurant on Alamy Street. Last week I made a **sioenervrat** for dinner, but when we arrived at the restaurant, our table wasn't ready. When we eventually sat down, the **everisc** was slow and the **nagwiti** staff were rude. When the food eventually arrived, the **rotniops** were tiny (all right if you are on a **tide**, but not so good if you're feeling hungry). My chicken was **rudecodnoke** (in fact it was still red on the inside!), and my partner's steak, which she wanted **earr**, was so **lewl-neod** that it was almost **trunb**! When the **kcech** arrived at the end of the meal, we discovered that we had been **hogvdeacrer** by almost $20. We refused to pay the **evsirec ragceh**, and naturally we didn't leave a **pit**.*

20

For reference see *Easier English Intermediate Dictionary* (0-7475-6989-4).

Hotels

Look at this extract from a hotel information leaflet and complete the gaps with words or expressions from the box. One word must be used twice.

advance   all-inclusive (AI)   amenities   bed and breakfast (B+B)
business and conference   cashiers   chain   chambermaids   charged   check-in
check-out   chefs   competitive   double   en-suite   experience   facilities   family
full-board   guests   half-board   housekeeping   Internet   non-residents   occupancy
options   pay-to-view   peak period   pool   quote   rates   receptionists   reservations
residents   room service   safety deposit   self-catering   shuttle   single   staff   suite
supplement   training   transfer   twin   uniform   vacancies   vacated   waiters
waitresses   website

Five Pillars Hotel, Cherryville, FL

The following room (1) _____ apply from April to October (prices are per person per night):

- (2) _____ room (1 single bed): $50
- (3) _____ room (2 single beds): $35
- (4) _____ room (1 King-size bed): $30 (+ single person (5) _____ (6) _____ of $20)
- (7) _____ room (1 King-size bed, 2 single beds): $35 (adults) $20 (children)
- (8) _____ (Bedroom, living room, bathroom): $65

All rooms are (9) _____ (attached bathroom with bath, shower and WC)

Special group (10) _____ are available for groups of 15 or more.
Call us for a (11) _____ (the number is at the bottom of this page)

Room (12) _____ include:
- Mini bar.   ■ (13) _____ box.   ■ Tea and coffee making facilities.   ■ (14) _____ satellite TV.   ■ Wi-Fi (15) _____ connection.

Hotel (16) _____ include:
- Restaurant and bar (open to (17) _____ and (18) _____).
- 24-hour (19) _____ (light meals only between 11.30 p.m. and 6.00 a.m.).   ■ Heated outdoor (20) _____.   ■ (21) _____ center.

For reference see *Easier English Intermediate Dictionary* (0-7475-6989-4).

The following meal-plan (22) _____ are available:

- (23) _____ (*European Plan*: room only. Cooking facilities provided)
- (24) _____ (*Bermuda Plan*: includes room + morning meal)
- (25) _____ (*Modified American Plan*: includes room, morning + evening meals)
- (26) _____ (*American Plan*: includes room + all meals)
- (27) _____ (Includes room, all meals, snacks, tea, coffee and other drinks)

Note that the hotel is very busy during our (28) _____ between June and August, so (29) _____ (30) _____ are essential. We recommend that at other times you telephone first to see if there are any (31) _____.

Also please note that earliest (32) _____ time is 2.00 p.m., and the latest (33) _____ time is 11.30 a.m. All rooms must be (34) _____ by this time, or (35) _____ will be (36) _____ for an extra night.

If you are arriving or leaving by air, the hotel operates a free airport bus (37) _____ service; (38) _____ time from the airport to the hotel is approximately 40 minutes.

The Five Pillars Hotel is part of the *Elite* (39) _____, with over 75 hotels and motels throughout the USA and Canada. Call 0119 ELITEYU for more information, or visit our (40) _____ at www.luvelite.com.

JOBS ✳ JOBS ✳ JOBS ✳ JOBS ✳ JOBS

Are you interested in working for any of the Elite hotels? We are always looking for new (41) _____. Here are just a few of the areas you could work in. No previous (42) _____ is necessary, as full (43) _____ will be given. We will offer you a (44) _____ salary and provide you with a (45) _____. Contact us on the number above.

- Cleaners and (46) _____ to work in our busy (47) _____ departments.
- (48) _____ to meet and greet our customers when they arrive.
- (49) _____ and (50) _____ to work in our popular restaurants and bars.
- (51) _____ to prepare quality meals in our kitchens.
- (52) _____ to run our exchange bureaus and handle the financial side of the hotel

For reference see *Easier English Intermediate Dictionary* (0-7475-6989-4).

Job advertising

Exercise 1:

Match the words and expressions in the first box with one of the dictionary definitions in the second box.

(1) advance   (2) application   (3) basic salary   (4) benefits   (5) candidate   (6) colleagues   (7) commencing   (8) commission   (9) cover letter   (10) drive (*noun*)   (11) experience   (12) incentive   (13) increment   (14) interview   (15) leading (*adjective*)   (16) motivate   (17) post (noun)   (18) qualified   (19) relocation allowance   (20) responsibilities   (21) résumé   (22) rewards package   (23) team   (24) vacancy

A.   To have the right qualifications.
B.   Money which is given to a sales person for selling a certain amount of goods (usually expressed as a percentage of the value of goods sold).
C.   To encourage somebody to do something.
D.   Something which encourages you to work harder.
E.   The different things you need to do as part of your job.
F.   A letter that you send with a résumé, document, etc., which gives basic information about why you are sending it.
G.   (In a job) To reach a higher position with more money and more responsibility.
H.   The collection of different things that you receive in return for doing your job.
I.   The people you work with in a company.
J.   A job.
K.   A detailed list of your qualifications, work experience, etc.
L.   The knowledge and skills that you get by doing a particular job.
M.   A job which is not filled by somebody.
N.   The things that you get for doing your job in addition to money.
O.   The minimum amount of money you receive for doing a job.
P.   A group of people who work together in one company or department.
Q.   The questioning of a person who is applying for a job.
R.   Money which is sometimes paid to somebody when they leave one place to go and work in another place.
S.   A formal request (usually written) for a job.
T.   A more formal word for *beginning* or *starting*.
U.   The most successful or most important.
V.   A regular pay rise, often based on how well an employee performs at work.
W.   An energetic way of working.
X.   A person who applies for a job.

Exercise 2:

Look at this conversation and complete the gaps with words or expressions from Exercise 1. Try to do this *without* looking back at Exercise 1.

Bob: What are you reading?

Terry: The jobs pages in the paper.

Bob: Oh really? Anything interesting?

Terry: Well, there's something here I like the sound of. Modus International, a (1) _____ supplier of auto parts, has a (2) _____ for the (3) _____ of Sales Manager in their Seattle office.

For reference see *Easier English Intermediate Dictionary* (0-7475-6989-4).

Bob: That sounds like your kind of job. When does it begin?

Terry: Let me see. Er, (4) _____ April 1st, it says here. That's in three weeks' time.

Bob: You'd better get your (5) _____ in, if you're interested. What else does it say about the job?

Terry: It says that the successful (6) _____ should be suitably (7) _____ and should have had extensive (8) _____ in sales management.

Bob: That sounds perfect. You've got a University degree in Business Management, and you've been working in sales for more than five years.

Terry: I guess so. It also says that he or she should be able to work as part of a (9) _____, and should have (10) _____ and the ability to (11) _____ and inspire his or her (12) _____.

Bob: Well, that's great! You've always got on with the people you work with, and everyone is always saying how you're able to encourage people to work harder.

Terry: That's true. It also says that the (13) _____ include liaising with colleagues around the country, training new staff and presenting a full report to the board of directors twice a year.

Bob: It all sounds quite good. What's the company offering in return?

Terry: The (14) _____ they're offering looks very attractive. It includes a (15) _____ of $35000 per annum…

Bob: What does that mean?

Terry: Well, that's the minimum amount of money that you can earn during the year. In addition to that, they're offering 10% (16) _____ on all sales made.

Bob: Well, that's a good (17) _____. The more you work, the more you sell. And the more you sell, the more money you'll make!

Terry: Exactly. There's also a guaranteed annual (18) _____ of $2500, and a (19) _____ of $4000.

Bob: What's that for?

Terry: To pay me for moving to the area, finding an apartment, and so on. Oh, and there are other (20) _____, such as a company car, free medical and dental insurance and free meals in the cafeteria. It also says that there is room to (21) _____, so I might end up with an even better job within the company.

Bob: So what should you do if you're interested in applying for the job?

Terry: It says I should send my (22) _____, together with a (23) _____, to their head office in Los Angeles. If the company is interested, they'll contact me to arrange an (24) _____ at one of their offices nearer home.

Bob: Go for it! I can come and visit you. I've always wanted to see the Pacific Ocean!

Also see *Contracts* on pages 12 and 13, *Earnings, rewards and benefits* on pages 16 and 17, and *Job recruitment* on pages 25 and 26.

For reference see *Easier English Intermediate Dictionary* (0-7475-6989-4).

Job recruitment

Look at the pairs of words and expressions in **bold** in this article, and decide which one is best in each situation. In several cases, *both* words are correct.

Part 1

When a company has a (1) **vacancy / vacant** for a job, and it needs to (2) **hire / recruit** a new member of (3) **crew / staff**, it usually (4) **publicizes / advertises** the (5) **post / position**. It does this (6) **internally / internationally** (for example, in the company magazine or on a company notice board, so that the job is only open to people already working for the company), or (7) **extensively / externally** in the 'situations vacant' section of a newspaper. It might also use a recruitment (8) **agency / agenda**, which helps people to find (9) **job / work**.

A job advertisement has to give an accurate (10) **describing / description** of the job and what the company needs and expects from the (11) **applicant / application** (the person who is (12) **applying / appalling** for the job). These (13) **requirements / requisitions** might include (14) **qualifications / qualities** (academic, vocational or professional), (15) **experience / experiences** in similar lines of work, and personal (16) **qualifications / qualities** (for example, it might say that you need to be (17) **practicing / practical**, (18) **professional / professorial** and have a sense of humor).

Most advertisements specify the (19) **rewards / remuneration** that the company can offer in return for your work (including the basic annual (20) **wage / salary**, any commission you could receive, regular pay (21) **rises / increments**, and so on). Some advertisements will also tell you about other (22) **benefits / beneficial** (including paid annual (23) **leave / vacations**, free medical care, a company car, free meals in the cafeteria, etc.) that you might receive. If the (24) **packet / package** they are offering is very generous and attractive, and is (25) **commensurate / commendable** with the work that is necessary, the company can expect a lot of people to apply for the job.

Part 2

If somebody is interested in the job, they are usually asked to send to send their (1) **resume / résumé** with a (2) **cover / covering** letter. Alternatively, they might be asked to (3) **fill in / fill out** an (4) **application / applicant** form and (5) **submit / send** it to the company. The managers of the company will read these and then make a (6) **short-list / small-list** of the people it wants to (7) **attend / attempt** an interview. At the same time, it will (8) **reject / turn down** those who it feels are (9) **unsuitable / unthinkable**.

For reference see *Easier English Intermediate Dictionary* (0-7475-6989-4).

During and after the interviews, the managers will consider the different aspects of the (10) **candidates / applicants** to decide whether they have the correct (11) **potency / potential** for the job. These might include physical (12) **apparition / appearance** (are they smart and well-presented?), general (13) **disposition / disposal** (for example, are they friendly and easy to work with?), special (14) **skills / abilities** (for example, are they computer literate, can they drive, or do they speak any other languages?) and (15) **interests / hobbies** (what do they like doing in their free time?). They might also consider their family (16) **backing / background** (are they married, do they have children?) and (17) **medicine / medical** history. The person who most closely (18) **suits / matches** the (19) **profile / criteria** decided by the managers will then be accepted for the job.

Before somebody is (20) **offered / suggested** the job, s/he is asked to provide (21) **referees / references** from people who know him / her (usually a former (22) **employer / employee**, a (23) **colleague / co-worker**, and / or a close friend). Before s/he actually starts working, s/he may go through an (24) **induction / introduction** program to learn more about the company and the job. Sometimes, s/he may be given a (25) **temporary / temporal** contract and obliged to complete a (26) **trial / probationary** period (where his / her employers make sure that s/he is suitable for the job) before being offered something that is more (27) **permanence / permanent** (a fixed-term or open-ended contract, for example). After s/he has been with the company for a while, there will probably be an (28) **appraisal / appreciable**, to assess how s/he is getting on. These may be repeated on a regular basis throughout his / her time with the company.

Also see *Contracts* on pages 12 and 13, *Earnings, rewards and benefits* on pages 16 and 17, and *Job advertising* on pages 23 and 24.

For reference see *Easier English Intermediate Dictionary* (0-7475-6989-4).

Addition, equation and conclusion

If you take the TOEIC® Test of Spoken English, you might be asked to give a recommendation, state your opinion about something or describe the cause and / or effect of something. Your language will flow more naturally and your ideas will be clearer if you are able to 'join' your ideas together using conjunctions such as *and*, *so*, *because*, *but*, etc., and other expressions.

Each of the paragraphs below contains a gap. This gap can be completed with one *or more* of the words or expressions below each paragraph. Decide which of them can be used.

1.   Visitors to another country should respect the local environment. _____ they should respect the local customs.
     (A) **Therefore**   (B) **Likewise**   (C) **Similarly**   (D) **In the same way**

2.   _____ bringing much-needed money to developing countries, tourism provides employment for the local population.
     (A) **Besides**   (B) **In the same way**   (C) **As well as**   (D) **In addition to**

3.   Tourism brings much-needed money to developing countries. _____, it provides employment for the local population.
     (A) **Furthermore**   (B) **In addition**   (C) **Along with**   (D) **Moreover**

4.   The company lost a large share of its market to a competitor. _____, it had to close down two of its factories.
     (A) **Consequently**   (B) **Likewise**   (C) **Because of**   (D) **As a result**

5.   The acting in the movie was terrible, the story was boring and the sound quality was very poor. _____, I wouldn't recommend it to anyone.
     (A) **In brief**   (B) **So**   (C) **In the same way**   (D) **Correspondingly**

6.   When we made a loss for the third year in a row, two hundred factory workers lost their jobs _____ half the sales department.
     (A) **together**   (B) **also**   (C) **along with**   (D) **similarly**

7.   During the war, many young men went abroad to fight. _____ the number of children being born dropped sharply during this period.
     (A) **For this reason**   (B) **Consequently**   (C) **Besides**   (D) **Since**

8.   Economic activity in the area has declined _____ poor government investment.
     (A) **because of**   (B) **due to**   (C) **as a result of**   (D) **on account of**

9.   _____ my home town is mainly industrial, there is very little reason for tourists to visit it.
     (A) **Thanks to**   (B) **Because of**   (C) **Owing to**   (D) **Seeing as**

10. 'The Clockwork Gallery' toy museum is not only popular with children: it is popular with adults _____.
     (A) **as well**   (B) **too**   (C) **also**   (D) **in addition**

11. _____ offering a generous salary and other benefits, the company received very few applications for the job.
     (A) **In spite of**   (B) **However**   (C) **Despite**   (D) **Nevertheless**

12. There is only one hotel in the town and it is always full. _____, if you want a room there, you should book well in advance.
     (A) **Therefore**   (B) **However**   (C) **Due to**   (D) **Consequently**

For reference see *Easier English Intermediate Dictionary* (0-7475-6989-4).

Location and direction

Where is the **movie theater** on the map on the next page? Work it out by reading sentences 1 – 26 below, and matching the roads, buildings and other places mentioned with the letters (A, B, C, etc.) on the map. The movie theater is not actually mentioned in any of the sentences, so you will have to use deduction and a process of elimination to find it. The sentences are in no particular order.

1.   Stallone Street runs alongside the railway line.
2.   Clemenceau Avenue connects Dominion Street with Central Avenue.
3.   Easy Street is a one-way street.
4.   Central Avenue runs through the middle of the town, parallel to Dominion Street.
5.   City Hall faces Washington Park.
6.   If you want to get to the library from City Hall, the best way is to cross Dominion Street, walk through Washington Park to Central Avenue, and walk west along Central Avenue until you get to Commercial Street. You'll find the library at the far end of Commercial Street.
7.   To get to the department store from the library, cross over Commercial Street and walk toward Central Avenue. You'll see the department store on your left.
8.   There is a deli on the corner of Central Avenue and Telegraph Road.
9.   You cannot drive your car along Commercial Street: it is a pedestrian-only zone.
10.   The post office is at the intersection of Commercial Street and Central Avenue.
11.   The nightclub is next to the fast food restaurant.
12.   There is a tourist information office on Stallone Street directly opposite the railway station.
13.   Washington Park is surrounded on all sides by roads.
14.   The bus station is directly across the road from the tourist information office.
15.   The railway station is in the south-east of the town.
16.   To get to the Grand Hotel from the station, the best way is to cross Stallone Street, walk along Telegraph Road and at the end of the road turn left onto Central Avenue. Take the second road on your right, and you'll find the hotel at the far end of this road.
17.   The safest way to get to Washington Park from the art gallery is to use the pedestrian underpass that goes under Clemenceau Avenue.
18.   Park Lane is at right angles to Central Avenue.
19.   The fast food restaurant is at the end of Dominion Street, where it meets Easy Street and Park Lane.
20.   The nightclub is on Park Lane.
21.   Commercial Street and Telegraph Road are parallel to each other, but at opposite ends of the town.
22.   The museum is adjacent to the post office.
23.   The shopping mall is to the west of City Hall, just past Marlene's bar.
24.   To get from the bus station to Luigi's restaurant, go along Telegraph Road, and turn left at the intersection. The restaurant is the first building on your left.
25.   The Grand Hotel is diagonally across Dominion Street from City Hall.
26.   Marlene's bar is between City Hall and the shopping mall.

For reference see *Easier English Intermediate Dictionary* (0-7475-6989-4).

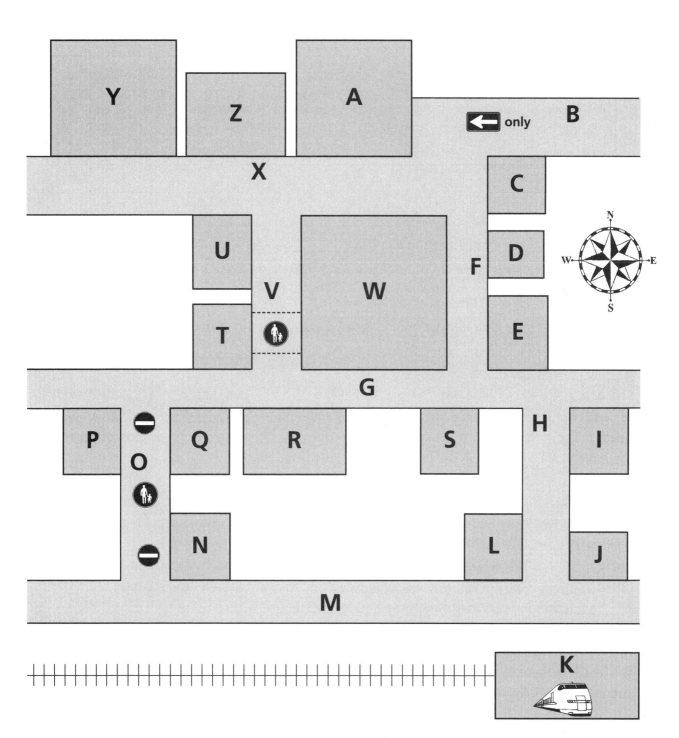

Look at sentences 1 – 26 again, and <u>underline</u> or *highlight* the key words and expressions of *location* and *direction* that helped you to navigate your way around the map. Make a note of these words and expressions, and try to make them an active part of your vocabulary.

For reference see *Easier English Intermediate Dictionary* (0-7475-6989-4).

Meetings and presentations

Look at this opening address from a company's Annual Meeting and fill in the gaps with words from the box. The first letter of each word is already in the text.

-articipants	-atters	-bjectives	-chedule	-chieve	-ddress	-ecommendations
-elcoming	-eport	-et through	-genda	-hair	-inutes	-larification	-loor
-loses	-nterrupt	-oals	-oints	-omplaints	-ontribute	-otes	-pen
-pen-floor	-pinions	-ringing up	-riority	-rogress	-ssues	-ttendance
-uestions	-ummarizing	-upporting				

Mr. Roberts:

I'd like to (1) **o**_____ this meeting by (2) **w**_____ you all. It's good to see so many (3) **p**_____ here today – in fact, this is probably the best (4) **a**_____ we've had at a meeting for a long time – and I'd like to thank you all in advance for (5) **s**_____ me.

Well, we've got a lot on the (6) **a**_____ and I want to make as much (7) **p**_____ as possible in the next two hours or so. If we stick to the main (8) **s**_____, we should (9) **g**_____ everything and
(10) **a**_____ all of our (11) **g**_____ and (12) **o**_____. I will (13) **c**_____ the meeting, as usual, but I really hope that you will all have something to (14) **c**_____, and if anything needs (15) **c**_____, please don't hesitate to (16) **i**_____ me (although not too often, I hope: the more (17) **i**_____ we can (18) **a**_____ today the better).

I'll be (19) **b**_____ several important (20) **m**_____ during the meeting, beginning with those that I feel should take (21) **p**_____, before (22) **s**_____ the main (23) **p**_____ and making
(24) **r**_____. This will be followed by an (25) **o**_____ session where you can give me your
(26) **o**_____. And I'm sure you will all be delighted to hear that after the meeting (27) **c**_____, there will be drinks and snacks for everyone.

Mr. Barker will be taking (28) **n**_____ and keeping the (29) **m**_____ of the meeting, and I will be using these to write my (30) **r**_____ afterwards, so if anyone has any (31) **c**_____, I suggest you talk to him and not to me!

Now, before I get going, are there any (32) **q**_____ from the (33) **f**_____?

Everyone else at the meeting:

Zzzzzzzzz

For reference see *Easier English Intermediate Dictionary* (0-7475-6989-4).

Exercise 1:

Explain the differences between the words and expressions in **bold** in the following groups.

1.   To **lend** and to **borrow**
2.   **Inflation** and **deflation**
3.   A **discount** and a **refund**
4.   **Income** and **expenditure**
5.   To be **insolvent** and to be **bankrupt**
6.   A bank **statement** and a bank **balance**
7.   To be **in the red** and to be **in the black**
8.   An **invoice** and a **receipt**
9.   To make a **profit** and to make a **loss**
10. **Gross** profit and **net** profit
11. To be **undercharged** and to be **overcharged**
12. Something which is **overpriced** and something which is **exorbitant**
13. To **save** money and to **invest** money
14. A **wage** and a **salary**
15. **Extravagant** and **economical**
16. A **loan** and a **mortgage**
17. A **loan** and an **overdraft**
18. **Shares** and **stocks**
19. **Commission** and **interest**
20. Something which is **worthless** and something which is **priceless**
21. To **credit** and to **debit**
22. A **pension** and **redundancy pay**
23. A **dividend** and a **royalty**
24. **Tax** and **duty**
25. To **deposit** money and to **withdraw** money
26. A **bill** and a **check**

Exercise 2:

Complete these paragraphs with appropriate words or expressions from Exercise 1. In some cases you will need to change the form of the word, and in some cases more than one answer may be possible.

1.   The store is happy to exchange faulty goods, but it can only offer customers a _____ on production of a valid _____.
2.   Customer: Excuse me, waiter. I think you've _____ me. This _____ says that my pizza cost $30.50.
     Waiter: That's correct sir. It's $25, plus a service charge of 10%, and government _____ of 12%.
     Customer: Well I think that's an _____ price to pay for a pizza!
3.   This month's bank _____ shows that we have an _____ of $800. We can't afford to be _____ to such a large amount. It's time we reduced our _____.
4.   Our sales representatives receive a basic _____ (pre-tax) annual _____ of $20,000, plus a 10% _____ for each item they sell. On average, their _____ (post-tax) _____ is around $45,000 a year.
5.   The company was declared _____ after it was unable to pay off all its debts. Many people who lost their jobs as a result did not receive _____, and those who were about to retire lost half of their _____. People who had _____ heavily in the company saw their _____ become completely _____.

Also see *Money matters 2* on pages 32 and 33, *Earnings, rewards and benefits* on pages 16 and 17, and *Shopping and consumerism* on pages 47 and 48.

For reference see *Easier English Intermediate Dictionary* (0-7475-6989-4).

Money matters 2

Complete sentences 1 – 28 with a word or expression related to money, and write your answers in the crossword grid on the next page. Some of the letters have already been put into the crossword grid. However, to make it more challenging for you, there are no numbers in the grid, and the sentences below are in no particular order!

Note that in some cases, more than one answer may be possible, but only one will fit into the accompanying space in the crossword grid.

1.   The US dollar is very weak at the moment, so fewer people can _____ to take a vacation overseas.
2.   Payment can be made by cash, _____ or credit card.
3.   The company _____ the bank almost $2 million, which it is currently unable to pay back.
4.   Thank you for your order. Your goods have been despatched, and the sum of $17.50 will be _____ from your account within the next five days.
5.   Last year we paid too much tax (over $10,000 too much in total), so this year we hope to get a _____ for the same amount.
6.   Aviva Ltd is happy to offer new customers interest-free _____ for the first six months. After that, an interest rate of 18% will apply.
7.   The sale begins next week. Customers can expect some fantastic _____, including a flat-screen home cinema package for less than $500.
8.   Most people who lose their jobs end up on _____, although many say they are too embarrassed to receive government handouts.
9.   The _____ of living goes up every year. This is partly due to inflation, and partly due to increased taxation.
10.   The city hopes to start building a new library next year, provided it can get government _____ to begin the project. The minimum amount it hopes to receive is $750,000.
11.   The US dollar is a hard _____ and can be easily exchanged for those from other countries.
12.   The company's _____ are handled by an accountant from the one of the city's biggest financial firms.
13.   The company has lost a lot of money recently, and may be forced to sell some of its _____, including the company jet and two office blocks in Manhattan.
14.   The airline will offer passengers up to $500 _____ for lost luggage or damage to personal property.
15.   Before you start your own company, it is essential to have enough _____ to start it up and keep it running until it begins to make a profit.
16.   The city has an excellent public transport system which is _____ by local government so that it can keep its fares low.
17.   The latest art exhibition to be shown at the Metropolitan is a collection of photographs and paintings of chocolate. Not surprisingly, it is being _____ by the country's biggest chocolate manufacturer, Hoggychocs.
18.   We have invested over $2 million in the company, but unfortunately the _____ has been very low and we are considering selling our stocks.
19.   I didn't think the project would make us much money, but in fact it was extremely _____, and we made over $30,000!
20.   My job doesn't pay very well. In fact, my _____ are not enough to pay the rent.
21.   Many people think that all writers make a _____ from their books, but unfortunately this is rarely true.
22.   The computer costs $1500, but you do not need to pay for it all at once: you can make a _____ (2 words) of $200, and pay for the rest later.
23.   We have increased our publicity _____ by $600,000, giving us a total of over $3 million to spend on advertising.

For reference see *Easier English Intermediate Dictionary* (0-7475-6989-4).

24. Every year the company's accounts are checked carefully for any mistakes. This annual _____ also helps us to identify areas where we could improve our sales record.
25. Our _____ are rapidly increasing. Last month they were $20,000, and this month they are $32,000. I don't know how we're going to pay them off.
26. If your order costs over $50, delivery is free of _____.
27. If you make a reservation in advance, the hotel can offer you a special _____ of $65 a night, including breakfast.
28. When the dollar is strong it can buy more foreign _____, which means that more people are inclined to travel abroad.

Also see *Money matters 1* on page 31, *Earnings, Rewards and benefits* on pages 16 and 17, and *Shopping and Consumerism* on pages 47 and 48.

For reference see *Easier English Intermediate Dictionary* (0-7475-6989-4).

Obligation and option

Complete sentences 1 – 17 with a suitable word from the box. More than one answer is possible in some cases.

alternative	compelled	compulsory	entail	essential	exempt	forced	have	liable
mandatory	must	need	obligation	obliged	optional	required	voluntary	

1.   A valid passport and visa are _____ by all visitors to the country. Unless you have these, you will not be allowed in.

2.   The wearing of helmets and safety clothing on site is _____. You may not enter the site without these.

3.   Note to hire car drivers: all passengers _____ wear seatbelts. This includes rear-seat passengers. Your insurance will be invalid if you fail to comply.

4.   There are no direct flights between London and New Orleans. Passengers flying between these cities _____ to change in New York or Washington.

5.   All companies are _____ for the health and safety of their employees while on company premises, and can face heavy financial penalties if they fail to comply.

6.   Because of the recession, several companies in the area have been _____ to close.

7.   Books, clothes and food are currently _____ from government tax, as they are considered necessities rather than luxuries.

8.   _____ safety inspections are carried out twice a year. Companies should allow government safety inspectors complete access to all areas.

9.   Entrance to the museum is free, but visitors are asked to make a _____ donation of $5.

10.   There is no service charge in this restaurant, but we do ask that groups of 8 or more pay an _____ 10% extra.

11.   Unless you make prompt repayments, we will have no _____ but to reclaim the property from you.

12.   Manufacturers of packaged foods are _____ to list all the ingredients clearly on the box or package. This should include any artificial colorings and additives

13.   You are under no _____ to work overtime, but we hope that you would be prepared to work late at least once a week.

14.   When Mr. Smith made a mistake that cost his company over $100,000, he felt _____ to leave and look for work elsewhere.

15.   The project is very exciting, but everyone realizes that it will _____ a lot of work.

16.   You can order our latest software programs by phone or online. And the great thing is, there's no _____ to pay until you've received your purchases.

17.   It is absolutely _____ that deliveries are made on time, otherwise we will start to lose customers.

For reference see *Easier English Intermediate Dictionary* (0-7475-6989-4).

Opposites 1: verbs and adjectives

Complete the sentences below with an opposite of the verb or adjective in **bold**, then write the words in the appropriate space in the table. If you do this correctly, you will reveal two more words in the shaded vertical strips that are opposites of each other. (Note that in some cases, more than one answer may be possible, but only one will fit into each space in the table.)

1. A project can **fail** or it can _____.
2. An object can be **solid** or it can be _____.
3. A job can be **temporary** or it can be _____.
4. A metal edge (on a knife, for example) can be **blunt** or it can be _____.
5. You can **reward** somebody for good behavior, or you can _____ them for bad behavior.
6. There are some things you can say in **private** that you should never say in _____.
7. A surface can be **rough** or it can be _____.
8. Calculations can be **exact** or they can be _____.
9. You can **lend** something to somebody, or you can _____ it *from* somebody.
10. In a court of law, a person can be found **innocent** or they can be found _____.
11. You can **postpone** a meeting to a *later* date, or you can _____ it to an *earlier* date.
12. In an accident, you might suffer from a **major** injury or a _____ one.
13. A pool of water can be **deep** or it can be _____.
14. **Professional** sports people can make a lot of money, but _____ ones do it for fun or pleasure.
15. Some students in the class were **absent**, but most of them were _____.
16. Some foods contain **natural** flavorings, but many contain _____ ones.
17. You can either _____ or **reject** an offer.
18. You can **create** something or you can _____ it.
19. You can **admit** doing something wrong, or you can _____ it.

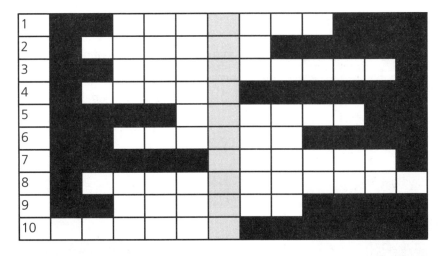

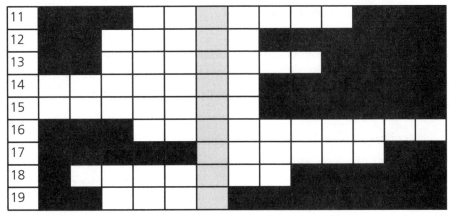

For reference see *Easier English Intermediate Dictionary* (0-7475-6989-4).

Opposites 2: Adjective prefixes

A lot of adjectives can be made into their opposite form by adding a *prefix* (*un-*, *in-*, *dis-*, *il-*, etc.) to the beginning of the word.

<u>Task 1</u>: Decide which of the prefixes from the first box can be used to make opposites of the words in the second box.

dis-	il-	im-	in-	ir-	un-

acceptable   accurate   adequate   advantaged   agreeable   attractive
authorized   avoidable   believable   certain   comfortable   competent
complete   conscious   contented   convincing   correct   curable
even   fair   fashionable   honest   inclined   legal   limited
literate   logical   married   mature   moral   mortal   obedient
organized   patient   perfect   personal   possible   proper
pure   qualified   rational   regular   relevant   replaceable   resistible
resolute   responsible   satisfactory   satisfied   sufficient   welcome

<u>Task 2</u>: Without looking at your answers to Task 1, look at the following sentences and paragraphs. In each one there is one word which has been given the wrong prefix. Decide which word is wrong and correct it.

1. He is a very (A) <u>disagreeable</u> man and he makes visitors feel very (B) <u>unwelcome</u>, but the management think he's (C) <u>irreplaceable</u> and are (D) <u>uninclined</u> to fire him.

2. Insider dealing is not only (A) <u>immoral</u> and (B) <u>inhonest</u>, but also (C) <u>illegal</u>: companies are legally bound to take the strongest possible action against such (D) <u>unacceptable</u> behavior by their employees.

3. It is an (A) <u>unavoidable</u> fact, but in a competitive job market, those who are (B) <u>unqualified</u> or who have (C) <u>imsufficient</u> work experience will find themselves seriously (D) <u>disadvantaged</u>.

4. She was described by her boss as being (A) <u>unresponsible</u>, (B) <u>incompetent</u> and (C) <u>immature</u>, which she considered extremely (D) <u>unfair</u>.

5. In return for an increased investment, the company offered (A) <u>unlimited</u> returns for their investors. While many found such an offer (B) <u>irresistible</u>, some thought the promises were (C) <u>innconvincing</u> and were (D) <u>uncomfortable</u> about parting with so much money.

6. He had clearly given his presentation (A) <u>disadequate</u> preparation, and many in the audience challenged the points he made, saying they were (B) <u>inaccurate</u> and (C) <u>illogical</u>. Despite this, he remained (D) <u>irresolute</u> in his views, although the only person he managed to convince was himself.

For reference see *Easier English Intermediate Dictionary* (0-7475-6989-4).

Opposites 3: verb prefixes

Some verbs can be made into their opposite form, or otherwise modified, by the addition of the prefixes *dis-, im- mis-* or *un-*.

Complete each of the sentences below with one of the prefixes above and the *most appropriate* verb from the box. In most cases, you will also need to change the end of the verb (by adding -s, -ed, -ing, etc., and in some cases by also removing a letter). Use your answers to complete the crossword on the next page.

agree	allow	approve	behave	calculate	connect	continue	cover
diagnose	fold	judge	like	load	lock	obey	place	please	prove
qualify	quote	represent	trust	understand	use			

Across

2. The press have once again _____ the President: he said that women were 'America's hope for the future', and not 'America's hopeless future'.
3. The National Patients' Association is calling on Senators around the country to make doctors legally responsible for _____ an illness.
6. Despite recent rumors in the press, Kaput Computers is pleased to announce that it will *not* be _____ its popular line of budget laptops.
8. The press deliberately tried to _____ our company, wrongly suggesting that we plan to sell arms abroad.
10. Deliveries need to be _____ from the truck as soon as they arrive, and placed in the storeroom on the first floor.
12. If any employee _____ with the new working regulations, they should speak to their line manager.
13. If any employee _____ the company computers (eg, by sending personal emails or for accessing undesirable websites), they will be instantly dismissed.
14. Getting nowhere in your job? Then _____ the secrets to business success with our new book, 'The Only Way is Up!'.
16. As the full extent of the company's financial problems _____, the management decided to take drastic action.
20. Employers have every right to _____ interview candidates who are not able to provide adequate references or show proof of their qualifications.
22. The management _____ of employees smoking during working hours.
23. Some staff members have _____ several directives regarding punctuality, and can expect to be disciplined.

Down

1. We completely _____ the time we had for the project, and unfortunately we were unable to finish on time.
2. Overseas business deals sometimes fail when one party _____ the other's intentions, usually as a result of linguistic or cultural differences.
4. It is dangerous to remove paper jams in the photocopier without first _____ the copier from the power supply.
5. New government legislation has been criticized for offering compensation to people who have been _____ from driving and who have lost their jobs as a result.
7. The lack of progress has _____ the management, and in view of this they plan to review working procedures.
9. The salesman accidentally _____ the discount due to us, so we hardly broke even on the deal.

For reference see *Easier English Intermediate Dictionary* (0-7475-6989-4).

11. It is a sad fact of office life that when the manager is away some employees feel free to _____.

15. The company claimed $20,000 for fire damage, but the claim was _____ because proper safety procedures had not been observed.

17. We regret that our trust in your company was sadly _____, and therefore we will not be dealing with you in the future.

18. A recent company investigation has _____ several cases of unauthorized Internet use during office hours.

19. The huge increase in exports recently has _____ the argument that the world has stopped buying American goods.

21. Unfortunately, many of our employees _____ the new uniform, claiming it is old-fashioned and uncomfortable.

For reference see *Easier English Intermediate Dictionary* (0-7475-6989-4).

Ownership, giving, lending and borrowing

Rearrange the capital letters in **bold** in these sentences to make nouns and verbs related to ownership, giving, lending and borrowing. Write these words in the grid. If you do this correctly, you will reveal a word in the shaded vertical strip that can be used to complete the sentence at the bottom of the page.

1. **ROTPEPYR** prices in the city center have doubled in the last five years. As a result, many companies are choosing to set up in the suburbs, where land and buildings cost up to 40% less.

2. Calling all **RDOLDLSAN**! Do you have houses and apartments that are still empty? Do you want to fill these with reliable, trustworthy city workers and get a decent price? Then call 'Rooftops' agency today!

3. Our department has been **COALTELAD** $5,000 to buy new furniture and computers.

4. Employees will be **VOPDRIED** with a uniform, which they should wear at all times when dealing with members of the public.

5. When you buy real estate you will need to take out a **GMTOERAG**, unless you have enough money to pay for it.

6. Entrance to the museum is free, but we ask visitors to make a small voluntary **ATIDNONO** of two or three dollars to help pay for its upkeep.

7. Guests are reminded that the hotel is not responsible for the loss of or damage to their personal **ISSSSSEPONO**, and are advised to keep any valuables in the hotel safe.

8. Our company doesn't actually own the building we operate from. It's owned by Bigbucks Holdings Ltd, and we're just the **NETSNAT**.

9. Before we could start trading, we had to get a $100,000 **ONAL** from the bank to pay for the license and begin our advertising campaign.

10. Food at the party was free, but everyone was asked to **TIRCNUTOEB** $5 to pay for the drinks.

11. The shop is owned by the city council, but it is **ESEADL** to a British company which sells sports equipment.

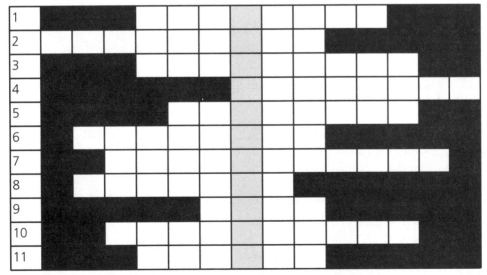

The word you should reveal in the shaded vertical strip can be used to complete this sentence:

_____ of small, independent stores in towns and cities often complain that they are unable to compete with major stores and malls in the suburbs.

For reference see *Easier English Intermediate Dictionary* (0-7475-6989-4).

Phrasal verbs 1

Phrasal verbs are very common in English, and should be learnt like any other item of English vocabulary. They may appear at any stage in the TOEIC®. The exercises on the next 3 pages give you practice in some of the most common and useful phrasal verbs.

Complete the sentences below with a phrasal verb comprising a *verb* and *one or two particles* from the box. The meaning of the phrasal verb is explained in parentheses at the end of each sentence. In some cases, you will need to change the form of the verb (eg, to past simple, present continuous, third-person 's', etc.). In each sentence, the phrasal verb has one more letter than the previous sentence (ie, the phrasal verb in number 1 has 4 letters, in number 2 it has 5 letters, in number 3 it has 6 letters, etc.).

> against   away   call   come   cut   fill   do   end   forward   get   go (x2)   look
> of   off (x2)   out (x2)   pull   run   subject   through (x3)   to (x3)   up (x3)   with (x2)

1.   Prices are expected to _____ by 20% next year. (*to rise / increase*)

2.   Unless we reduce the amount of energy we use, we'll _____ getting a huge bill at the end of the next quarter. (*to finish in a certain situation without wanting or intending to*)

3.   We were in the middle of negotiations on the phone when we were suddenly _____. (*to have a phone call stopped before it is finished*)

4.   When you _____ the application form, don't forget to include a daytime telephone number. (*to write information in the empty spaces on an official document*)

5.   Unless we act soon, we'll _____ options. (*to have nothing left*)

6.   When the chairman heard about the deal, he _____ it _____. (*to decide not to do something*)

7.   If the country decides to _____ customs inspections for goods from Canada, it may lead to the market being flooded with surplus goods. (*to get rid of something / remove something*)

8.   The company was _____ a lot of very difficult questions regarding its operating methods. (*to make somebody or something experience something unpleasant*)

9.   We had to _____ them the importance of keeping a proper filing system. (*to make someone understand – usually with difficulty – something important*)

10.   A lot of companies complain that they often _____ unnecessary bureaucracy and red tape when dealing with foreign companies. (*to have to deal with something difficult, often without expecting it*)

11.   The economic recession almost destroyed a lot of smaller businesses, but thanks to government funding, many are now _____. (*to recover*)

12.   After looking carefully at the potential advantages and disadvantages of a merger, the directors eventually _____ it. (*to do something you have planned to do*)

13.   We are very much _____ doing business with you. (*to be happy about something that will happen in the future*)

For reference see *Easier English Intermediate Dictionary* (0-7475-6989-4).

Complete the phrasal verbs in **bold** below with appropriate particles (in, out, up, etc.). In each sentence, the particles you need are the same. Each of the phrasal verbs in number 10 needs 2 particles.

1. We are **counting** _____ you for your support, and we are also **relying** _____ you to keep us informed of the latest developments, otherwise we are not sure we will be able to **go** _____ working with you.

2. At the meeting, the manager **pointed** _____ that after he had **worked** _____ the overall cost of the project, he had **figured** _____ we would need to **pull** _____ of the deal.

3. While attempting to **set** _____ its Miami department and **build** _____ its customer base in the area, the company **ran** _____ debts of almost $20 million.

4. Global Travel Ltd cannot afford to **put** _____ the issue of redundancy any longer: the international economic recession has **set** _____ a series of problems, and the travel industry has **come** _____ particularly badly.

5. Before AVC Motors **took** _____ the running of Varsie's Autos, it **went** _____ its list of assets very carefully, but it failed to **look** _____ the business premises.

6. When management-union talks **broke** _____ and the production lines had to be **shut** _____ as a result, the people who had worked so hard to make the negotiations a success felt they had been badly **let** _____.

7. During the union dispute, the management said that they would rather **hand** _____ their notice than **give** _____ to union demands, but in the end they decided to **call** _____ an independent arbitrator to deal with the unrest.

8. If enough people **show** _____ at tomorrow's meeting, I would like to **bring** _____ the subject of pay increases: business has **picked** _____ a lot recently, and I think it is only fair that our staff our rewarded.

9. The company **ran** _____ some unexpected financial difficulties, and when the accounts department **looked** _____ the problem carefully, they discovered that a computer hacker had **broken** _____ their files and stolen almost $2 million.

10. In order to **catch** _____ _____ our competitors and **keep** _____ _____ market developments, we will need to **put** _____ _____ increased production costs.

Now try using the phrasal verbs above in some of your own sentences.

Make sure you use the phrasal verb in its correct form, paying particular attention to the tense of your sentence (for example, present continuous, past simple, present perfect, etc.).

Don't forget to keep a written record of any new phrasal verbs you learn, and try to review and use them regularly so that they become an active part of your vocabulary.

For reference see *Easier English Intermediate Dictionary* (0-7475-6989-4).

Phrasal verbs 3

Each of the following paragraphs uses 4 phrasal verbs in **bold**. However, one phrasal verb in each paragraph is incorrect because the wrong particle (*in, out, on*, etc.) has been used. Identify and correct that particle in each case.

1. I **came across** the plans while I was **going up** some old files. I wanted to **throw them out**, but my boss told me to **hold on to** them in case they might be useful in the future.

2. The flight departure was **held up** because a group of tourists were late **checking into**, and by the time we eventually **took off**, it was **getting on for** 11 o'clock.

3. We need to **tighten up** security in the workplace, so over the next few months a series of new security measures will be gradually **phased in**. We're **bringing in** a firm who specialize in this field, and we're hoping they will **come up to** a workable program.

4. The company is **looking into** the possibility of opening a department in China to **deal with** the growing market for our products in the country. If we **go ahead** with this, we will then need to **build about** a reliable network of suppliers and carriers in the region.

5. We might have to **face up to** the fact that the deal with Automart might **fall up**. I've asked the committee to **check out** other options available to us if this happens, but we might have to **fall back on** our original plan.

6. The company is going to **bring apart** some of the best minds in the industry to **carry out** a survey looking at the possibility of expanding the company into Europe. They will then **put together** a series of measures and options available to us. Our main concern at the moment is how to **get round** the inevitable bureaucracy that will be involved.

7. I expect there will be a few problems, but these can probably be **smoothed out** without much difficulty. I must **put across** to everyone my view that we have no intention of **dropping in of** the project at this stage, and I suggest we **go about** this exciting challenge with enthusiasm and determination.

8. Because of economic difficulties, the company has **come under** severe financial pressure. This means that we need to **cut back on** staff in several departments, and so over the next two years, several positions will be gradually **phased out**. The unfortunate task of informing those who will have to leave **falls for** Ms. Bailey, our Human Resources manager.

9. We hold regular staff training and development sessions after work which all employees have to **take part in**. Nobody can **opt out of** these unless they have work commitments. And the management become very suspicious if employees try to **get out of** any of the sessions by suddenly **coming through** with mystery 'illnesses'!

10. Although he **came in** a lot of money when his father died, he decided to **carry on** working for the company. He enjoyed his work so much that he **turned down** the offer of promotion. However, he decided to leave when he **fell out** with his boss over plans to make several of his colleagues redundant.

11. The staff all **look up to** the company Director: he's efficient, he's approachable and he's friendly. He **looks after** them like they were his own children, and is always happy to **sort out** any problems that they might have. In that respect, he **takes to** his father, who started the company in 1987.

12. When she didn't **turn round** for work for the third day in a row, we decided to **find out** what the problem was. It **turned out** that she was unhappy in her job because she felt the boss was always **picking on** her and making her life difficult.

For reference see *Easier English Intermediate Dictionary* (0-7475-6989-4).

Each of the sentences below contains a missing preposition. Four possible answers follow the sentence. Choose the best answer in each case.

1. The next monthly meeting is _____ 2 April.
    (A) **on** (B) **at** (C) **in** (D) **with**

2. Your completed application form must arrive _____ 2 October at the latest.
    (A) **in** (B) **at** (C) **during** (D) **by**

3. The company has been running its Houston office _____ the beginning of 2003.
    (A) **for** (B) **at** (C) **since** (D) **in**

4. Mrs. Lebrowski is my boss: I've worked _____ her for five years.
    (A) **over** (B) **between** (C) **through** (D) **under**

5. Traveling _____ Europe by train is a wonderful and unique experience.
    (A) **by** (B) **across** (C) **at** (D) **on**

6. The hotel is happy to provide its guests _____ soap, shampoo and other toiletries free of charge.
    (A) **with** (B) **for** (C) **under** (D) **during**

7. The average commuter journey _____ work takes 47 minutes.
    (A) **by** (B) **to** (C) **at** (D) **on**

8. The duty manager is responsible _____ dealing with any problems that customers have.
    (A) **about** (B) **with** (C) **against** (D) **for**

9. All office paperwork has to be filed: don't throw anything _____.
    (A) **down** (B) **out** (C) **up** (D) **over**

10. The night train _____ Washington, D.C. arrives in Miami early the next morning.
    (A) **by** (B) **with** (C) **at** (D) **from**

11. Commuters rely _____ a punctual, comfortable and safe public transport service to get them to work.
    (A) **on** (B) **for** (C) **about** (D) **to**

12. The seminar has been moved from Wednesday _____ Friday.
    (A) **until** (B) **for** (C) **to** (D) **by**

13. Employees who are repeatedly absent _____ work for no reason will have their wages reduced.
    (A) **about** (B) **with** (C) **at** (D) **from**

14. I always have a big evening meal, but for some reason I always wake up hungry _____ the middle of the night.
    (A) **at** (B) **on** (C) **in** (D) **to**

15. The quickest way to get from New York to Chicago is _____ air.
    (A) **by** (B) **on** (C) **in** (D) **through**

16. Your pay claim has to be approved _____ the financial comptroller before she can give you any money.
    (A) **at** (B) **for** (C) **to** (D) **by**

17. The shopping mall has been running a very popular car valet service _____ two months.
    (A) **before** (B) **for** (C) **since** (D) **in**

18. I was so tired that I slept _____ most of the movie.
    (A) **through** (B) **in** (C) **between** (D) **to**

19. The manager is on a training course in Denver and will be back _____ a few days.
    (A) **in** (B) **at** (C) **since** (D) **until**

20. Most Americans would rather stay home and watch TV _____ the evening than go out.
    (A) **on** (B) **in** (C) **at** (D) **to**

For reference see *Easier English Intermediate Dictionary* (0-7475-6989-4).

Prepositions 2

The sentences below each contain four <u>underlined</u> prepositions. One of the prepositions is not correct. *Identify* and *correct* that preposition in each sentence.

1. Your new job will require you to travel all (A) <u>over</u> the world (B) <u>with</u> business, and you will have to work (C) <u>with</u> some difficult people (D) <u>in</u> some very boring places.

2. The seminar, which will be held (A) <u>from</u> 9 o'clock and midday (B) <u>in</u> the Lincoln Conference Hall, will be presented (C) <u>by</u> Adam Klaus, an expert (D) <u>on</u> recent IT trends.

3. Following a series of advertisements (A) <u>in</u> the local paper, over 100 people applied (B) <u>on</u> the position of Exports Coordinator, and the Manager set himself the task of personally replying (C) <u>to</u> every one (D) <u>by</u> the end of the week.

4. We're meeting (A) <u>with</u> a very important client (B) <u>in</u> half an hour, so I'm afraid I'm (C) <u>over</u> a lot of pressure (D) <u>at</u> the moment.

5. The office is open Monday (A) <u>through</u> Friday (B) <u>from</u> 8.30 a.m. (C) <u>to</u> 5.30 p.m., but it is closed (D) <u>at</u> Wednesday afternoons.

6. The report is due (A) <u>on</u> Monday morning, but it doesn't have to be presented (B) <u>to</u> the board of directors (C) <u>by</u> Wednesday afternoon, when they arrive (D) <u>for</u> the annual meeting.

7. The flight doesn't arrive (A) <u>in</u> Los Angeles (B) <u>until</u> midnight, so once passengers have collected their luggage (C) <u>from</u> the luggage reclaim and gone (D) <u>up</u> customs and immigration, public transportation will have stopped running for the night.

8. He complimented me (A) <u>on</u> my hard work, thanked me (B) <u>for</u> the help I had given him, wrote his email address (C) <u>at</u> the back of one of my business cards and asked me (D) <u>to</u> contact him when I got home.

9. Most workers go (A) <u>with</u> bus or subway (B) <u>from</u> the suburbs (C) <u>to</u> the city center, but sometimes it is quicker to go (D) <u>on</u> foot.

10. The chairman sat (A) <u>between</u> the manager and the union leader and did his best to answer questions (B) <u>from</u> the workers, although there were several angry employees (C) <u>among</u> them who did their best to prevent him (D) <u>for</u> speaking.

11. The airline apologized (A) <u>for</u> the extended delay, told the passengers they were grateful (B) <u>about</u> their patience, and offered (C) <u>to</u> return part of their fare or give them a discount (D) <u>on</u> their next flight.

12. The city is famous (A) <u>for</u> its beautiful architecture, is rich (B) <u>in</u> history and culture, and has a population who are justifiably proud (C) <u>for</u> their heritage and who always offer a warm welcome (D) <u>to</u> visitors.

13. If guests are not satisfied (A) <u>with</u> the service they receive any time (B) <u>during</u> their stay, they should speak (C) <u>to</u> a customer advisor, or alternatively discuss their problems (D) <u>at</u> the duty manager.

14. International travelers often suffer (A) <u>from</u> minor stomach upsets when they are (B) <u>on</u> vacation, but this is usually the result of a sudden change (C) <u>for</u> their diet rather than poor standards of hygiene (D) <u>in</u> the kitchen.

Note that in the error recognition section of the TOEIC®, you are required to *recognize* the error in each sentence, but unlike the exercise above you do not have to correct it.

For reference see *Easier English Intermediate Dictionary* (0-7475-6989-4).

Sales and marketing

Exercise 1:

In the following sentences, the owner of a cell phone company is telling people about his company's latest model of cell phone. However, each sentence contains a spelling mistake. Identify and correct the word in each case.

1. Everybody says that the market for cell phones is very cowded, and there is no more room or demand for new products.

2. However, we believe we've found a nich in the market for something a little bit different: a cell phone that lets you smell the person you're talking to! Wow!

3. We call it the 'Smell-O-Phone®', and you can find it in our latest brocure, along with some of our other models.

4. It's the ultimate must-have opmarket accessory.

5. We made the decision to start making it after extensive reserch into what people wanted from a cell phone in the 21st century.

6. Of course, we won't sell many without a great deal of advertiseing.

7. As a result, we're launching a major campain to let the public know all about it.

8. We're going to premote the Smell-O-Phone® any way we can.

9. There are going to be comercials on all of the main radio stations and television channels.

10. And advertisments in all the daily newspapers and major magazines.

11. You won't be able to walk down the street without seeing one of our giant billyboards.

12. And you won't even be able to visit the Internet without our plop-ups coming up on your screen all the time!

13. We're also going to send mailshoots to everyone who has ever bought one of our phones in the past.

14. And naturally we'll be making some sponsership deals with some of the country's major sporting teams.

15. If we're lucky, we might even get a famous rock star, actor or sports personality to endoarse it for us.

16. There will also be big posters at every pont of sale (including department stores and music stores).

17. In fact, there probably won't be a single major retale outlet anywhere in the country that doesn't sell the Smell-O-Phone®!

18. Our expert salesmen will be there to give potential customers their pich and persuade them that the Smell-O-Phone® is just what they need.

19. There will be lots of special offers, including disconts on phone and talk-time packages.

20. There will also be lots of giveways: free hands-free kits, free phone covers, free ring tones, and so on.

21. Sales won't just be limited to the dommestic market.

22. We believe that the *Smell-O-Phone*® will really catch on in the expot market as well.

23. In fact, our overseas raps are already packing their suitcases and booking their flight tickets.

24. Eventually we hope to have the *Smell-O-Phone*® made under franshise in Europe, the Far East and South America.

25. You might also like to know that in addition to the phone itself, there will be a whole range of *Smell-O-Phone*® merchantising, including *Smell-O-Phone*® T-shirts, *Smell-O-Phone*® trainers and even *Smell-O-Phone*® candy!

26. They will all carry the famous *Smell-O-Phone*® brant.

27. And come in a unique *Smell-O-Phone*® pakaging.

28. Check out our latest cattalog to see the whole range!

29. We think it's the best invention since the microchip, although obviously some people will tell you that it's just hyp, and we're making a lot of fuss about nothing.

30. They'll say that the *Smell-O-Phone*® is nothing more than a fat, and that this time next year nobody will want one!

31. However, I just know it will sell well, and I bet our competiton is getting really worried!

32. Perhaps I can canvince you to buy one? Go on! You know it's just what you've always wanted!

33. Hmm, I can see you're somebody who is going to need a lot of perswading!

Exercise 2:

Match these dictionary definitions with some of the key words in exercise 1. These key words will be the ones that you corrected.

1. A detailed list of products or services, often with pictures, prices, etc.

2. To say publicly that you support something or approve of it.

3. The box or packet that a product is sold in.

4. The place where a product or service is sold directly to the public.

5. The things that somebody says to encourage you to buy something.

6. Something that is very popular for a short time.

7. An excessive claim in advertising.

8. The people or companies who sell a similar product or service as you, and who want to do better than you.

9. The name of a well-known product (for example, Nike, McDonald's, etc.)

10. A reduction in price on a product or service.

11. Giving money to a group or organization in exchange for the right to advertise at events, on clothes, etc.

12. Information that a company sends by post to lots of people who might want to buy their product or service.

13. More expensive, appealing to the wealthy section of the market.

14. Send goods abroad / to another country.

Also see *Shopping and consumerism* on pages 47 and 48.

For reference see *Easier English Intermediate Dictionary* (0-7475-6989-4).

Shopping and consumerism

Complete these sentence pairs with the most appropriate word or expression in **bold**. In several cases you will need to change the form of the word (for example, by making it plural or changing the tense).

1.   **chain / concession**
     (A) We don't have our own stores, but we operate _____ in several major department stores across the state.
     (B) I. B. Conningyou is the most successful _____ store in the state, with almost 30 outlets in 12 cities.

2.   **consumer / customer**
     (A) The store is very popular and is always full of _____.
     (B) Electronic _____ goods such as hi-fi's, televisions, computers and cameras can be bought very cheaply on the Internet.

3.   **cost / charge**
     (A) Despite a fall in oil prices, some gas stations are still _____ drivers too much for their gas.
     (B) Many people are surprised to learn that it doesn't _____ a lot to set up your own website.

4.   **spend / pay**
     (A) A lot of people _____ too much money on fast food when there are far healthier options available in the stores.
     (B) The company _____ a lot for its new computers, but believes it has been worth the investment.

5.   **credit / debit**
     (A) The store is happy to offer regular customers instant _____ at an attractive APR of only 13.5%.
     (B) Thank you for buying your camera from EasyCameras.com. The sum of $220 will be _____ from your account within 5 working days.

6.   **offer / discount**
     (A) Prices in most stores are fixed, but it is often possible to ask for a / an _____.
     (B) Would you like a brand-new laptop for only $300? If you want to take advantage of this amazing _____, then hurry to PCPerfect now!

7.   **exchange / change**
     (A) Please check your _____ carefully before leaving the store, as mistakes cannot be rectified later.
     (B) Jade Furnishings Ltd will only _____ damaged goods if they were damaged before they left the store.

8.   **price / cost**
     (A) It is usually cheaper to buy electronic goods on the Internet, where _____ are generally lower than in the stores.
     (B) A lot of stores have been forced out of business because their _____ (including rent, electricity and staffing) is too high.

9.   **retail / wholesale**
     (A) The disks usually cost 50 cents each in the stores, but we buy them _____ direct from the manufacturers for 20 cents each.
     (B) If you go to the store, the _____ price is $250, but it can be up to 40% cheaper if you buy online.

10. **for sale / on sale**
     (A) The building is _____ for $600,000.
     (B) For all your office equipment needs, come to Berkshire and Hunt, where you will find a large range of products _____.

For reference see *Easier English Intermediate Dictionary* (0-7475-6989-4).

11. **receipt / bill**
(A) When you pay, make sure that the shop gives you a _____: you will need this if you have to return goods at a later date.
(B) Customers are reminded that all _____ must be paid within 5 working days.

12. **check / bill**
(A) That meal was delicious! Shall we ask the waiter for the _____ now?
(B) Can I pay you with a $50 _____? I'm sorry I don't have anything smaller.

13. **charge / check**
(A) You can pay by cash or _____.
(B) The advantage of paying with a _____ card is that you don't have to pay for your goods immediately.

14. **economic / economical**
(A) Buying something in large quantities direct from the manufacturer is much more _____ than buying from a store.
(B) Because of the ongoing _____ situation, we regret that we will cease trading on 15 March.

15. **supply / stock**
(A) The item you have requested is currently out of _____, and we do not expect any further deliveries for two weeks.
(B) Hanratty's Food Stores are a major chain who _____ the catering industry with the finest and freshest meat, fruit and vegetables.

16. **serve / service**
(A) The manager was unhappy when he learnt that some of his customers had to wait 15 minutes to be _____.
(B) Fordley and Mantle are very proud of the quality of _____ they offer their customers.

17. **demand / supply**
(A) Prices often go up when _____ for a product rises.
(B) Prices often come down when _____ of a product increases.

18. **purchase / merchandise**
(A) The store has a large range of designer _____ available to the public at very low prices.
(B) Although New York is a popular shopping destination, visitors tend to limit their _____ to one or two major items.

19. **return / refund**
(A) We regret to announce that we can only _____ 75% of the original price of your goods if you are unhappy with them.
(B) If you need to _____ anything to us, please make sure it is well-wrapped and you have paid sufficient postage.

20. **team / staff**
(A) If you have a query, please ask a member of _____.
(B) The store has done well because it has an excellent management _____.

21. **make / do**
(A) Nowadays, most people _____ their shopping in large malls outside the city.
(B) The company _____ so much money that it was able to set up a chain of stores across the country.

Also see *Sales and marketing* on pages 45 and 46.

For reference see *Easier English Intermediate Dictionary* (0-7475-6989-4).

Similar meanings 1: nouns

Being familiar with words and expressions which have a similar (or the same) meaning to each other will give you a big advantage in the TOEIC®, especially in the Reading Comprehension section. The exercises on the next 6 pages give you practice with some of the most common and useful examples of these.

Exercise 1: Look at sentences 1 – 15. These can either be completed with a word from box A *or* a word with a similar meaning from box B. Identify both the words that could be used. In many cases, you will need to add an -*s* to one or both of the words when you put them into the sentence.

A	B
accommodation agenda appointment assistance benefit customer discipline discount drop fault opposition proof proximity requirement work	advantage client closeness decline defect employment evidence help housing meeting order prerequisite resistance reduction schedule

1. We have a very busy _____ / _____ today, so I suggest we start as soon as possible.
2. The company provides free _____ / _____ for its staff.
3. We need to maintain _____ / _____ on the factory floor at all times, otherwise there are increased risks of an accident occurring.
4. Thank you for your kind _____ / _____: I couldn't have done it without you.
5. There has been a sharp _____ / _____ in the number of people attending the staff development sessions.
6. The latest computer program has several _____ / _____ which need to be sorted out before it can be put onto the market.
7. There has been a lot of _____ / _____ to the new compulsory overtime plan.
8. There is no _____ / _____ to show that standards of living have improved.
9. Repeated orders are eligible for a 10% _____ / _____ on wholesale prices.
10. The hotel is popular with business people because of its _____ / _____ to the central business district.
11. I can't see you this afternoon because I have a / an _____ / _____ with the Board of Directors.
12. A lot of our _____ / _____ say that they are unhappy with the speed of our service.
13. When the company begins operations, it hopes to provide _____ / _____ for 300 people.
14. There are several _____ / _____ to working from home: you save on travel costs, for one thing.
15. If you want the job, a working knowledge of German is one of the main _____ / _____.

For reference see *Easier English Intermediate Dictionary* (0-7475-6989-4).

Exercise 2: Instructions as above

A	B
acclaim choice code cooperation customer liability outlet overview priority problem question revision staff strategy term	change collaboration complication condition (short) description option patron personnel plan praise precedence query responsibility rule store

1. His latest film has received widespread _____ / _____ and is expected to become a major box office success.

2. The company _____ / _____ state(s) that no employee can leave his or her work station without asking for permission.

3. The hotel accepts no _____ / _____ for any damage to vehicles in the car park.

4. There are two _____ / _____ available to us: close the company or move to another locality.

5. Our latest brochure provides a / an _____ / _____ of our latest products and a brief history of the company.

6. All _____ / _____ are requested to attend tomorrow's meeting, which will begin at 2 o'clock.

7. Thanks to our _____ / _____ with several affiliated companies, we have increased our turnover by 37%.

8. _____ / _____ are requested not to smoke in the restaurant.

9. We advise you to read the _____ / _____ of the contract carefully, and contact us if you disagree with any of the points covered.

10. If you have any _____ / _____, please ask a member of staff.

11. Selfwood's operates several _____ / _____ where you can buy a selection of our own goods along with a large range of branded varieties.

12. We had hoped that everything would run smoothly, but unfortunately there have been several _____ / _____.

13. Our _____ / _____ is to wait for prices to fall before putting the product onto the market.

14. Advertising is currently our main concern, and it should take _____ / _____ over everything else.

15. Is it necessary to make any _____ / _____ to the plan, or should we keep it as it is?

For reference see *Easier English Intermediate Dictionary* (0-7475-6989-4).

Exercise 3: Instructions as above

A	B
achievement advertising assignment caliber category charisma disparity ending entitlement notion proceeds proficiency review specialist ultimatum	accomplishment (personal) appeal classification difference earnings expert final demand idea intellect and ability job publicity right skill termination write-up

1. The restaurant has received several good _____ / _____ in the press, and is a firm favorite with visitors to the city.

2. Our latest model is excellent, but without adequate _____ / _____, we won't sell enough to cover production costs.

3. We believe that the new manager's lack of _____ / _____ will have a negative effect on sales.

4. The hotel has several room _____ / _____, including five family rooms and two honeymoon suites.

5. Poor long-term sales figures resulted in the _____ / _____ of the contract and the closure of two offices.

6. If you leave the company, you will lose your _____ / _____ to a share of the profits.

7. We would very much appreciate having somebody of your _____ / _____ working for us: you would be of great benefit to the company.

8. We called in a health and safety _____ / _____ to examine the building for any potential problems.

9. He was given the _____ / _____ of dealing with the press and keeping the public informed about new developments.

10. The new manager has a strange _____ / _____ that all employees are potentially dishonest.

11. She hasn't reached the required level of _____ / _____ in typing, and will have to repeat that section of the training course.

12. His promotion to director was a remarkable _____ / _____ for someone so young.

13. The bank gave us a / an _____ / _____: pay back the money or face immediate closure.

14. Despite several changes to the pay structure, there is still a _____ / _____ in pay between graduate trainees and non-graduates.

15. All _____ / _____ from the sale of the building will be re-invested in the company.

When you keep a written record of words that you learn, you might find it useful to put them into related groups. This would include putting words with the same or a similar meaning together. Remember that you should also record words in context (you should show how they work in a sentence with other words).

For reference see *Easier English Intermediate Dictionary* (0-7475-6989-4).

Similar meanings 2: verbs

Look at the words and expressions in **bold**, and think of a word which has the same or a similar meaning *in the same context*. Use these words to complete the crossword on the next page. In some cases, more than one answer may be possible, but only one will fit into the crossword.

Across

1. **Examine** accounts
2. **Account for** something that has happened
5. **Recover** lost money or property
6. **Advertise** a product
9. **Help** a customer
11. **Use up** all your resources
15. **Firmly state** your opinion
17. **Prevent** a strike from taking place
18. **Firmly tell** somebody your terms and conditions
19. **Acquire** or **get** information
21. **Have an effect on** someone or something
22. **Manage** or **organize** a department
24. **Produce** or **make** good sales of a product
25. **Choose** something
27. **Understand** or **achieve** something
29. **Tell** somebody about an event that has happened
31. **Quantify** the effect of something
34. **Forbid** smoking in a public place
35. **Give** information or instructions to your staff
36. **Confirm** something is true
38. **Widen** your area of operations
40. **Ask** somebody for advice
41. **Approve** of a decision
42. **Oblige** somebody to do something
43. **Give** or **take** a message to somebody
44. **Remove** something from a sum of money

Down

1. **Speak** to an audience
2. **Take** on new staff
3. **Give** a contract to a company
4. **Interrupt** somebody at work
7. **Check** facts to see if they are true
8. **Collect** information
10. **Replace** something with something similar
12. **Make** a process **go faster**
13. **Deal with** a problem
14. **Control** a process or activity
16. **Come to** an interview
20. **Make up for** something you have done wrong
23. **Book** a restaurant table
26. **Keep** something for future use
28. **Suggest** something without saying it directly
29. **Disclose** information to somebody
30. **Make** something **clearer**
32. **Examine** information in detail
33. **Settle** an argument or disagreement
37. **Finish** making plans for something
39. **Agree** to do something

For reference see *Easier English Intermediate Dictionary* (0-7475-6989-4).

For reference see *Easier English Intermediate Dictionary* (0-7475-6989-4).

Similar meanings 3: adjectives

Exercise 1: Match the words or expressions in **bold** in 1 – 24 with words from the box which have a similar meaning. You should use each word from the box *once only*.

compatible	disciplinary	disparate	diverse	efficient	exceptional	flexible	important
industrious	integral	inventive	legitimate	lengthy	mandatory	modern	nominal
obligatory	perceptive	profitable	prosperous	punctual	steady	tedious	voluntary

1. **Compulsory** safety inspections
2. A **very important** part of something
3. A **well-run and productive** department
4. Two **well-suited** organizations
5. **Compulsory** attendance at a meeting
6. A **long** meeting
7. A **creative** idea
8. A **significant** event
9. A collection of **unrelated** objects
10. A **wealthy** town
11. A **valid** reason for doing something
12. An **optional** dress code
13. A **constant and continuous** price rise
14. An **outstanding** performance
15. A **varied** program of events
16. **Easily changeable** working hours
17. A **lucrative** venture
18. **Punitive** action
19. A **boring** and **repetitive** job
20. A **prompt** start to a meeting
21. A **small** membership fee
22. An **observant** young man
23. A course of **contemporary** world studies
24. A **hardworking** staff member

Exercise 2: Instructions as above

abrupt	abundant	adequate	crucial	discourteous	enduring
extensive	inconsistent	inflexible	luxurious	narrow	outdated	overall
prospective	relevant	resolute	restricted	risky	rudimentary	scrupulous
	simple	thorough	thriving	vibrant	

1. A **lively** office atmosphere
2. A **basic** menu
3. A **determined** effort
4. **Very comfortable** accommodation
5. A **likely or possible** job applicant
6. **Limited and controlled** access to a building
7. A **flourishing** tourist industry
8. A product's **lasting** appeal
9. A **comprehensive** search
10. **Basic** knowledge
11. A **pertinent** question
12. **Enough** information
13. A **sudden** change of plan
14. **Old-fashioned** working practices
15. The **general** idea
16. A financially **dangerous** plan
17. **Plenty of** opportunities
18. A **small** profit margin
19. **Erratic** behavior
20. A **rigid** schedule
21. A **very important** meeting
22. A **full or very detailed** investigation
23. An **impolite** shop assistant
24. An **honest and fair** dealer

For reference see *Easier English Intermediate Dictionary* (0-7475-6989-4).

Starting and stopping

The box below contains 37 words and phrasal verbs related to *starting* or *stopping* something. You will find these by reading horizontally left to right (⇨) and vertically down (⇩) only. Try to find as many of these as possible, then use them to complete sentences 1 – 24. In many cases, these sentences can be completed with more than one of the words / expressions. In the case of the verbs, you will need to change the form of some of them (for example, by adding -ed to the end).

Note that in the case of phrasal verbs, the verb and the particle can be found directly next to each other (for example, *take off* will appear in the box as *TAKEOFF*).

```
D  A  B  O  L  I  S  H  A  S  E  T  O  F  F  B  C  D  E  F  G  D
I  I  N  C  E  P  T  I  O  N  C  L  O  S  U  R  E  H  I  J  K  E
S  L  T  O  D  M  T  U  R  N  D  O  W  N  N  Q  U  A  S  H  O  T
S  P  A  U  I  Q  R  E  S  T  I  D  I  S  M  I  S  S  U  V  P  E
U  T  K  T  S  W  K  S  X  Y  N  Z  S  U  S  P  E  N  D  A  U  R
A  A  E  B  C  A  I  T  C  D  I  E  S  H  U  T  D  O  W  N  L  C
D  K  O  R  O  T  C  A  S  B  T  R  E  F  E  M  B  A  R  K  L  E
E  E  F  E  N  E  K  B  U  A  I  A  G  H  I  J  F  R  K  L  O  A
P  U  F  A  T  R  O  L  P  C  A  D  D  M  R  N  I  I  O  P  U  S
H  P  C  K  I  M  F  I  P  K  T  I  E  F  E  S  R  S  Q  R  T  E
A  S  A  U  N  I  F  S  R  O  E  C  L  R  T  E  E  E  Q  V  W  X
S  Y  N  Z  U  N  Y  H  E  U  O  A  E  E  I  T  L  A  U  N  C  H
E  U  C  A  E  A  R  E  S  T  A  T  T  E  R  U  B  I  I  T  O  F
I  A  E  T  O  T  S  S  E  R  E  E  Z  E  P  A  N  T  D  Y  O
N  U  L  W  I  E  F  R  E  S  I  G  N  E  P  H  A  S  E  O  U  T
```

1. We _____ the contract with our suppliers when they repeatedly failed to deliver on time.

2. I can't find the document anywhere on my computer. I must have accidentally _____ it.

3. We had to cancel the project when the bank _____ and refused to lend us any more money.

4. Because of an _____ of food poisoning recently, the staff cafeteria will be closed until further notice.

5. The company was _____ in 2002, but had to _____ less than a year later.

6. Before _____ on a long journey, it is very important to make sure you have everything you need.

7. Several of the airline's crews told the press that they were concerned about the safety of its aircraft, but the airline's owner managed to _____ the story before it went public.

For reference see *Easier English Intermediate Dictionary* (0-7475-6989-4).

8.   As a result of increased security and a bigger police presence, crime has been almost completely _____.

9.   The store installed security cameras to _____ shoplifters, but without much success.

10.   We tried to _____ the manager from making changes to the company structure, but he said he had already _____ the first stage of the plan.

11.   Our latest mobile phone will be _____ onto the market next month, and we are confident that sales will rapidly _____.

12.   Following a series of minor workshop accidents, production was temporarily _____ while the machinery was checked for faults.

13.   I _____ photography as a hobby when I was 13, but by the time I was 15, I had already decided to make it my career.

14.   The new regulations will not all begin at once: they will be gradually _____ over the next two years. Meanwhile, the old overtime system will be gradually _____.

15.   Between its _____ in 1925 and its eventual _____ in 2002, World Film Studios made over 300 movies.

16.   The company _____ trading in 2004 because of poor sales and consequent financial troubles.

17.   Mr. Vettriano is 64, so I guess he'll be _____ soon. I think he'll miss working here, though.

18.   Secretary: "That's it! I've had enough of this place. I _____!"
        Manager: "Oh really? Well, I'm not going to give you the chance. You're _____!"

19.   They made an excellent offer, but we were obliged to _____ it _____ because we were working on too many other projects.

20.   Prices have risen rapidly over the last year, but last week the company announced a price _____; they have promised no more increases until April next year.

21.   Banana Computers no longer make the Banana 127V printer: it's been _____.

22.   When Congress _____ the old tax laws, smaller companies suddenly found themselves much better off.

23.   We have a lot of things to discuss at this meeting, so I suggest we _____ immediately with a report on last year's sales.

24.   Several problems have _____ recently as a result of moving our distribution warehouse: one of these is the slow despatch time for overseas orders.

Also see *Continuing, repeating and starting again* on pages 10 and 11.

For reference see *Easier English Intermediate Dictionary* (0-7475-6989-4).

Exercise 1:

Read this extract from a magazine article about travel, and choose the correct words or expressions in **bold**. Some of the words / expressions are wrong, some have the wrong form, and some have been spelt incorrectly. Note that in some cases, both answers are possible.

More people are traveling (1) **abroad / aboard** in the 21st century than ever before. Going away for a week or two's (2) **vacating / vacation** has never been easier, and the age of (3) **mass / massive** tourism has truly arrived! If you prefer the comforts of home and have never been away before, here's how it works.

If you enjoy the convenience of a (4) **packing / package** tour (where you pay for your flights, (5) **transfers / transits** to and from the airport, and (6) **acommodations / accomodations / accommodations** in advance), you simply go to the travel (7) **operator / agency**, pick up a (8) **brochure / catalog** or two, find a (9) **destiny / destination** and (10) **itinerary / itinerant** that suits you, and (11) **reserve / book** it. You then (12) **pay a deposit / make a down payment**, and pay the (13) **remainder / balance** closer to your travel date. Just before you (14) **leave / depart**, your tickets arrive and then you're away.

If you are an (15) **independence / independent** traveler who prefers more freedom and (16) **flexibleness / flexibility**, log on to the Internet, find a website that sells cheap flights, choose your (17) **departure / departing** date and return date, then pay the (18) **airfee / airfare**. You will then automatically have an (19) **a-ticket / e-ticket** logged with the airline. If you choose a hotel at the same time, your chosen hotel will automatically be informed of your (20) **booking / reservation**. You should also receive (21) **consternation / confirmation** of everything by email. Closer to the date of your (22) **trip / excursion**, some airlines will even let you (23) **check in / check-in** online, to save you from waiting in line for ages at the airport (24) **terminus / terminal**. (25) **Ticketless / Ticketfree** travel has eliminated the need for piles of unnecessary paperwork. It's all so easy!

Or is it? Here are just a few things that you ought to consider (and remember, this all has to be done before you even get to the airport!).

First of all, you will need to check your passport: have you got one, for a start, and is it still (26) **validated / valid**? Most countries will not let you in if your passport (27) **runs out / expires** within six months. Secondly, what about a (28) **visa / visor**? More and more countries require you to have one, and this will cost you money (and time and effort, too: in some cases, you have to present yourself in person at the country's (29) **emmbassy / embassy**). Thirdly, you will need to get (30) **traveler's checks / traveling checks** and / or foreign (31) **currancy / currency**: if you choose the latter, you need to check the (32) **exchange / changing** rate to make sure you are getting a favorable (33) **deal / bargain**, and then in most cases you will need to pay (34) **comission / commission / commision** to the bank who supplies it. Finally, have you got adequate (35) **insurence / insurance / insureance** cover, are your (36) **vaccinations / vaccinnations / vacinations** up to date, will your mobile phone work abroad, and have you made (37) **arrangments / arangements / arrangements** for someone to look after your cat and dog, and water your plants, while you are away? (*continued on page…*)

For reference see *Easier English Intermediate Dictionary* (0-7475-6989-4).

Exercise 2:

Without looking back at Exercise 1, complete these definitions with words from that exercise.

1.   A traveler who makes his / her own travel arrangements without needing help or advice from a travel agency is known as an _____ traveler.

2.   A ticket for a journey that is stored on a computer and not given to the passenger is called an _____.

3.   The money you pay for a flight is called an _____.

4.   _____ is a word that means 'in another country'.

5.   When large numbers of tourists visit a popular destination, this is called _____ tourism.

6.   _____ is money that you pay a bank or exchange bureau for changing your currency into another currency.

7.   The rate at which one currency can be exchanged for another currency is called the _____ rate.

8.   A _____ is an injection or other form of medical treatment which protects you from dangerous or unpleasant illnesses and diseases.

9.   A _____ is a building at an airport where planes arrive or depart.

10. A _____ vacation is a vacation where you pay for your flight, hotels, etc., in one go and before you leave.

11. When you _____, you show you are ready to get on a flight by giving your ticket to someone at the airport.

12. _____ is an adjective which means that a document is legal and can be used.

13. A _____ or _____ is an arrangement you make for a room in a hotel, a table in a restaurant, etc.

14. A _____ is a general word for a journey (usually for a short period of time).

15. When somebody tells you that something is certain (for example, they tell you that you definitely have a room in their hotel), we say that they send you _____.

Also see *Travel 2* on page 59 and *Hotels* on pages 21 and 22.

For reference see *Easier English Intermediate Dictionary* (0-7475-6989-4).

Complete these sentences with the most appropriate word or expression in **bold**. In some cases, more than one answer is possible.

1. (*At the airport. A check-in assistant is talking to a passenger*) I'm afraid your flight has been **canceled / delayed / crashed / bumped**. It won't be leaving for another two hours.

2. (*At the airport. An angry passenger is talking to her colleague*) I don't believe it. The airline has **diverted / overbooked / rerouted / postponed** our flight and have told me there are no more seats available for us. We'll have to wait for the next one.

3. (*A business executive is explaining why he prefers to fly business class*) Flying business class is much more expensive than flying **tourist / coach / economy / club** class, but it's much more comfortable and the food is better.

4. (*An announcement is being made at the port*) The ship will soon be ready for **embarkation / disembarkation / boarding / climbing**. Would passengers please ensure they have their tickets ready and proceed to the gate.

5. (*At the airport, an announcement is being made to passengers arriving on a flight*) Welcome to Heathrow Airport. Could we remind **transition / transitive / transitory / transit** passengers to wait in the lounge until their next flight is ready.

6. (*At the airport, an assistant is helping a passenger to find the right terminal for her flight from New York to Boston*) Terminal 1 is the terminal for international flights. You need terminal 2 for **domesticated / domestic / domesticity / domicile** flights.

7. (*At the station, a clerk is explaining ticket prices to a passenger who wants to visit a town and return on the same day*). A one-way ticket to Harrington costs $27.50. A **triangle-trip / round-trip / circle-trip / square-trip** ticket will cost you $42.

8. (*At the bank, a clerk is telling a customer why he can't take out any more money with his American Express card*). I'm really sorry, sir, but you have already exceeded your **profit margin / loyalty points / credit limit / commission rates**.

9. (*On an aircraft, the captain is talking to his passengers*) If you need anything during the flight, please do not hesitate to ask one of our cabin **staff / gang / team / crew**.

10. (*A radio announcement is being made for people traveling to a city for their job*) Bad news for **expatriates / commuters / immigrants / migrants**, I'm afraid. Traffic on the freeway is locked solid for 12 miles.

11. (*An article in a magazine is talking about air travel*) In a recent survey, Albion International Air Ltd was voted the world's favorite **carrier / airline / airliner / airways** for its punctuality, comfort, quality of in-flight catering and, of course, its standards of safety.

12. (*A travel agent is explaining insurance policies to a customer*) We advise you to take out our **comprehensive / adhesive / apprehensive / defensive** insurance policy which will cover you against all risks that are likely to happen.

13. (*A tour operator is announcing its new range of environment-friendly holidays*) **Eco-tourism / Environmental tourism / Responsible tourism / Green tourism** has become so popular recently that we have added this to our range of holidays.

14. (*A car hire clerk is helping a customer choose a vehicle*) The roads here are so bad and so full of holes that we very much recommend you hire a / an **MPV / sedan / SUV / station wagon**.

Also see *Travel 1* on pages 57 and 58.

For reference see *Easier English Intermediate Dictionary* (0-7475-6989-4).

Word forms 1: nouns from verbs

<u>Exercise 1</u>:

The verbs in the top box can all be made into nouns by removing and / or adding letters. Decide on the noun form of each verb, and then write it (in its noun form) in the appropriate section of the table, depending on the changes that are made to it. There are five words for each section of the table, and there are 10 words that do not fit into any section of the table.

consume   negotiate   provide   expose   choose   supervise   qualify   admire
persuade   fail   sign   argue   permit   refuse   apply   solve   emphasize
subscribe   disturb   scrutinize   attend   justify   expect   identify   require
coincide   criticize   recognize   warn   survive   acquire   assure   intervene   abolish
arrive   manage   expand   lose   recommend   maintain   determine   rehearse
respond   suggest   prohibit   consult   decide   notify   relax   produce   prefer
imply   behave   compete   promote

Remove 2 letters, then add 4 letters:	(Example: conclude ➜ conclude ➜ conclusion)
Remove 1 letter, then add 7 letters:	(Example: verify ➜ verify ➜ verification)
Remove 1 letter, then add 5 letters:	(Example: examine ➜ examine ➜ examination)
Remove 1 letter, then add 4 letters:	(Example: reduce ➜ reduce ➜ reduction)
Remove 1 letter, then add 3 letters:	Example: concentrate ➜ concentrate ➜ concentration)
Remove 1 letter, then add 2 letters:	(Example: disperse ➜ disperse ➜ dispersal)
Add 3 letters:	(Example: depart ➜ departure)

For reference see *Easier English Intermediate Dictionary* (0-7475-6989-4).

Add 4 letters:	(Example: improve → improve<u>ment</u>)
Add 5 letters:	(Example: confirm → confirm<u>ation</u>)

Exercise 2:

Now take the verbs from the box that did *not* fit into any of the sections above, change them into nouns and write them in the grid below (in the same order that they appear in the box). If you do this correctly, you will reveal a word in the shaded vertical strip that can be a verb and a noun *without changing its form*.

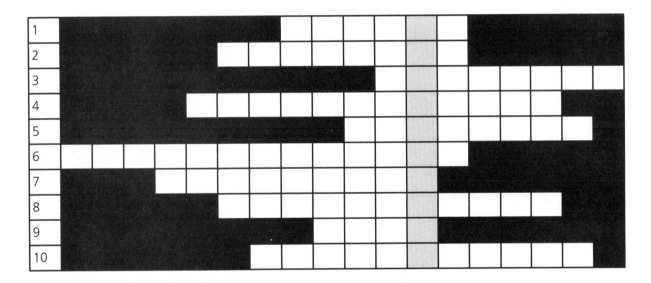

Now try using some of the words from this exercise in sentences of your own.

For reference see *Easier English Intermediate Dictionary* (0-7475-6989-4).

Word forms 2: nouns from adjectives

Exercise 1:

Look at these sentences and decide if the words in **bold** are the correct *noun* form of the *adjectives* which you will find at the end of each sentence. Correct those which are wrong. Look at the meaning of the whole sentence before you make any changes, and don't forget to check the spelling.

1. Items of **valuability** can be left in the hotel safe overnight. (*valuable*)

2. *La Poubelle d'Or* is the only restaurant in town for those with real **taste**! (*tasteful*)

3. Do you have a **thirstiness** for knowledge? Then why not enrol on one of our evening college courses? (*thirsty*)

4. It is often said that 'honestly is the best policy', which is why AZ Enterprises have adopted it as their company motto. (*honest*)

5. It can often be lack of **confidence** that prevents an employee performing well at work. (*confident*)

6. Many people who start up their own company are unaware of the **expensiveness** involved. (*expensive*)

7. Seniors can travel free on public transportation between 9 in the morning and 4 in the afternoon, although some **restrictions** apply. (*restricted*)

8. There are a few **similarties** between our old TZ18b model and the new TZ20. (*similar*)

9. The management are unable to say with any **certainence** when the new changes will be implemented. (*certain*)

10. Unnecessary **absentism** from work is costing American companies millions of dollars a year. (*absent*)

11. Please complete the form and return it at your earliest **convenientcy**. (*convenient*)

12. The union has questioned the **necessaryness** of downsizing, but the management insist it is the only way to keep the company going. (*necessary*)

13. Despite a **relaxation** of company rules regarding dress, many still prefer to wear a suit to work. (*relaxed*)

14. Sometimes in business, rules have to be changed according to needs: **flexiblence** is the key to success. (*flexible*)

15. Health and **safety** issues should be a priority with any organization. (*safe*)

16. The management accepts no **responsibleness** for items lost or stolen in the workplace. (*responsible*)

17. In advertising, **accurateness** is very important when it comes to identifying the target market. (*accurate*)

For reference see *Easier English Intermediate Dictionary* (0-7475-6989-4).

18. The legal **profession** is often criticized for concentrating on making money instead of upholding the law. (*professional*)

19. There have been unforeseen **complicatenesses** with our new building proposal owing to opposition from environmental groups. (*complicated*)

20. Do you know the **differents** between net profit and gross profit? Is *overtime* the same as *allowed time*? If you answered 'no' to the first and 'yes' to the second, it's time you joined our 'Business for Basics' course! (*different*)

Exercise 2:

Change the adjectives in the box into nouns following the instructions in the table. Each instruction relates to 3 of the adjectives in the box.

able   aggressive   appreciative   available   aware   bored   comfortable   compatible confused   considerate   convenient   creative   deep   familiar   fashionable   functional high   hot   logical   long   loyal   mature   optimistic   optional   pessimistic   popular punctual   realistic   secure   serious   strong   sufficient   systematic   true   warm   weak

Remove 4 letters:	
Remove 3 letters, then add 5 letters:	
Remove 3 letters, then add 1 letter:	
Remove 2 letters, then add 5 letters:	
Remove 2 letters, then add 3 letters:	
Remove 2 letters, then add 2 letters:	
Remove 2 letters:	
Remove 1 letter, then add 3 letters:	
Remove 1 letter, then add 2 letters:	
Add 2 letters:	
Add 3 letters:	
Add 4 letters:	

Try to use some of the words above in some of your own sentences.

For reference see *Easier English Intermediate Dictionary* (0-7475-6989-4).

Word forms 3: adjectives from verbs

Change the verbs in **bold** into their correct adjective form so that they are grammatically correct in the context of the sentences.

1. At the meeting we were shown a lot of **promote** material, but it wasn't very **inspire**.

2. Recently there have been some **innovate** and **impress** plans to change the working environment.

3. In the interests of the environment, our office staff need to change their **waste** habits, so we are introducing an **oblige** code for recycling and cutting down on waste.

4. The job was very **repeat** and as a result it quickly became very **bore**.

5. Everybody was very **excite** when we were offered the contract, but I was a little **doubt** it would go ahead.

6. Our new director isn't very **decide** and needs to play a more **act** role in the day-to-day running of the company.

7. Computer software designers need to be far more **invent** if they want to keep up with a changing and **change** market.

8. The photocopier has stopped working five times this week, and the air-conditioning hasn't been working for a month: these **continue** copier breakdowns, coupled with the **continue** heat, have resulted in a lot of short tempers.

9. The financial comptroller isn't very **approach**: in fact, some employees find him a little bit **frighten**!

10. Her argument wasn't very **convince**, and several of her colleagues were extremely **criticize** of her suggestions.

11. The market for all-**include** holidays (in which customers pay for their flight, accommodations, meals are drinks in advance) has become very **compete**.

12. Our boss is very **help** and **support**, but unfortunately he isn't very **depend**.

13. The mistake was easily **rectify**, but it would have been far more **prefer** if it hadn't happened in the first place.

14. Prices are non-**negotiate**, and you will need to pay a non-**refund** deposit of $500 before we can dispatch the goods.

15. There is **restrict** access to the building, and all visitors will need to show a **validate** pass and some form of ID.

16. Participation in the evening training seminars is entirely **volunteer**, but we hope that everyone will attend these highly **construct** sessions.

17. The accident was **avoid**, and it wouldn't have happened if you hadn't been so **care**.

18. He's a very **create** and **imagine** manager, and his track record is **admire**.

19. When you apply for a job, it is very important to be **specify** about your **occupy** qualifications, and any previous experience.

20. The job is full-time, and offers an **attract** salary and other **excel** benefits, including a company car and free healthcare package.

64

Workplace problems

In the following sentences and paragraphs, one of the words in each of the word pairs in **bold** is wrong and one is right. Identify the most appropriate word in each case. You will find this easier to do if you read each paragraph through first so that you have a better idea of what it is about. (Note that the wrong words are real English words, but do not fit into the context of the sentence / paragraph.)

Paragraph (A)

If there is a (1) **despite / dispute** between the management and the union in a company which cannot be (2) **restored / resolved**, and as a result a (3) **strike / stroke** looks likely, a third party might be called in to (4) **abdicate / arbitrate**.

Paragraph (B)

Poor (1) **timekeeping / timeserving**, persistent (2) **abstentions / absenteeism** and general (3) **misconception / misconduct** at work have lost us over $200,000 this year.

Paragraph (C)

Three managers have been accused of (1) **fraught / fraud**, (2) **dissemination / discrimination**, (3) **bullying / bumbling**, (4) **racy / racial** (5) **obtuse / abuse** and (6) **sectional / sexual** (7) **harassment / arrestment**. As a result two of them have been (8) **fried / fired** and one has been (9) **suspected / suspended** without pay. The first two are claiming (10) **unfair / unfaithful** (11) **dismissive / dismissal** and plan to (12) **appeal / appall**. The third has applied for a job with the government.

Paragraph (D)

We would like to point out that there have been several (1) **breaches / beaches** of the company's 'No smoking' policy. We also have proof that several factory floor workers have been (2) **neglecting / negotiating** their duties, and there have also been several incidences of (3) **insurrection / insubordination** towards senior managers and intentional (4) **damning / damage** of company property. If this happens again, those responsible will be taken before a (5) **disconcerting / disciplinary** (6) **broad / board** and could face (7) **instant / instance** (8) **dismal / dismissal**.

Paragraph (E)

The management are fully aware that because of staff (1) **shortness / shortages** we are all (2) **overstretched / oversubscribed** at the moment, Mr. Harrington, but we suggest that if you have a (3) **grievance / grievous**, you put it to us in writing rather than encourage your colleagues to hold a sudden (4) **walkout / walkabout**. We'd like you to treat this as a (5) **verbal / verdant** (6) **warming / warning**: the next time it happens, we will be obliged to ask for your (7) **notice / note**.

Paragraph (F)

What a terrible month! Sales have (1) **droned / dropped** by 40%, six employees have been made (2) **recumbent / redundant**, two senior managers have (3) **resigned / resided**, our main supplier has gone (4) **bankrolled / bankrupt**, someone has (5) **haggled / hacked** into the company website and given us a (6) **virus / viscous** (with the result that the entire computer system has (7) **crashed / cracked**), and the donut machine is *still* out of (8) **odor / order**.

For reference see *Easier English Intermediate Dictionary* (0-7475-6989-4).

Answers

1. widening   2. sharp decline / fall   3. general improvement   4. expansion   5. strengthening   6. tightening up   7. constant rise
8. dramatic increase   9. steady decrease   10. phased out   11. build up   12. cuts   13. deterioration   14. considerable growth
15. upward trend   16. marked progress   17. broaden (*to broaden your horizons* is an idiomatic expression which means to increase your ideas, knowledge and experience)   18. upgrade   19. streamline   20. Downsizing   21. slipped   22. fluctuated   23. amended
24. restructure

Changes 2 (page 3)

The words in the box are:
adapt replace expand increase promote reduce transform switch renovate exchange demote alter disappear vary raise lower extend enlarge heighten lengthen widen deepen shorten stretch revise fall outsource

1. exchanged   2. adapt   3. outsourced *or* switched (if you *outsource* a part of a company, you move part of the company operations from your home country to another country)   4. transformed   5. renovated   6. switched   7. vary   8. expanded   9. demote
10. revised (*revised* prices are usually increased, but they can also go down, as in this example)

Comparing and contrasting (page 4)

1. contrast   2. differ   3. differentiate   4. characteristics   5. distinction   6. Compared   7. comparison   8. resemble   9. similarities
10. In the same way   11. Likewise   12. By way of contrast   13. Nevertheless / Even so / However (*Even so* is more common in spoken than in written English)   14. discrepancy   15. whereas

Computers and information technology (I.T.) (pages 5 – 6)

Exercise 1:
1. desktop   2. laptop   3. components   4. CPU   5. hard drive   6. hard disk   7. memory   8. software   9. word processing
10. spreadsheet   11. DTP   12. load (we can also say *install*)   13. CD drive   14. USB port   15. flash-drive   16. monitor   17. keyboard
18. printer   19. scanner   20. mouse

Exercise 2:
1. Internet (sometimes also called *the World Wide Web,*or just *the Web*)   2. provider (also called an *Internet Service provider*, or *ISP*)
3. access   4. browser   5. download (if you transfer information from your computer to, for example, a website, you *upload* the information)   6. chatrooms   7. website   8. log on   9. pop-up   10. search engine   11. keywords   12. links   13. homepage
14. online (we often talk about *online shopping*)   15. log out   16. bookmark (it)   17. email (sometimes written *e-mail, Email* or *E-mail*. The *e* is short for *electronic*)   18. spam   19. delete   20. attachment   21. virus   22. crashing   23. upgrade (it)

Condition and requirement (page 7)

1. As long as   2. Unless   3. on condition that (*that* = optional)   4. providing that (*that* = optional. We can also say *provided that*)
5. precondition   6. In case of (note that in this particular expression, we do not say *In case of a fire*. In other situations, an article or pronoun would be needed after *in case of*)   7. In the event of   8. stipulation   9. unconditional   10. Assuming that (*that* = optional)
11. on the assumption that (*that* = optional)   12. prerequisites   13. terms / conditions   14. requirement   15. Failing that (*that* is needed here, as it refers back to the previous sentence. *Failing that* means that if the first option – *telephoning us* – is not possible, you should try the second option – *send us an email*)   16. otherwise

Confusing words (pages 8 – 9)

1. d   2. a   3. b   4. c   5. a   6. a   7. d   8. b   9. a   10. a   11. b   12. d   13. c   14. d   15. d   16. b   17. c   18. a   19. b
20. b   21. a   22. d   23. c   24. a   25. a   26. c   27. a   28. d   29. b   30. c

Continuing, repeating and starting again (pages 10 – 11)

Exercise 1:
1. ✓   2. resume (*restart* could also be used here)   3. ✓   4. revert   5. maintain   6. continual (Not *continuous*, as the computer sometimes works and sometimes doesn't. *Repeated* and *constant* could also be used here)   7. continuous (not *continual*, as the tone makes one long noise without stopping)   8. ✓   9. ✓   10. persevere (*press on* could also be used here)   11. perpetuate   12. ✓   13. reopen   14. keep up (*carry on* could also be used here)   15. persist   16. ongoing   17. ✓ (*continuous* could also be used here. A noise can also be described as *persistent* if it is repeated all the time: *the persistent ringing of a telephone*)   18. ✓ (*progress* could also be used here)   19. steady
20. ✓

For reference see *Easier English Intermediate Dictionary* (0-7475-6989-4).

1. repeatedly   2. continually   3. persists / carries on / continues   4. resume / restart   5. persevere   6. maintain   7. progressing / continuing   8. constant / continual / persistent   9. revert   10. Keep...up

Contracts (pages 12 – 13)

1.   1. parts = parties   2. False   3. C
2.   1. terminator = termination   2. True   3. obligated / required
3.   1. un-negotiable = non-negotiable   2. True (*amend* = change or alter. The noun is *an amendment*. You can <u>make</u> an *amendment*)   3. oral / spoken / implied / understood (Note that if a contract is on paper, it is called a *written contract*)
4.   1. in beach of = in b<u>r</u>each of (*breach* can also be a verb: *to breach a contract*)   2. abide by (in paragraph 1)   3. False (they have only breached one of the *clauses*, or *parts*, of the contract)
5.   1. period of notification = period of notice   2. agreement   3. True
6.   1. anointment = appointment   2. False (*amalgamation* comes from the verb *to amalgamate*: to join and become one. We can also say *merger*, from the verb *to merge*)   3. False (he is not allowed to have a *controlling interest* in the company, so his ability to buy stocks is restricted)   4. None (*third parties* are people or groups other than Mr. Wiley and the amalgamation of AKL Publishing and Berryhill Books)

Different situations (pages 14 – 15)

1. The speaker is explaining how to write a business / transactional letter.   2. They are at a conference.   3. Ms. Akkabar is a dentist.   4. False. He believes that *personnel training* and *development* are important (in order to maximize his employees' potential in the workplace   5. He's talking to someone (probably a receptionist) on the telephone: he wants her to connect him to another person in the building.   6. The speaker is talking about his company's *staff appraisal* program.   7. The speaker has a (very) bad boss!   8. Ms. Collins is explaining Mr. Sheppard's *duties* and *responsibilities* at work.   9. Mr. Sagala is a doctor (when we ask somebody how they *make their living*, we want to know what their job is).   10. They are looking at a bill or invoice for something.

Earnings, rewards and benefits (pages 16 – 17)

1. salary   2. remuneration   3. overtime   4. increment   5. deduction   6. minimum wage   7. double time   8. pension plan   9. raise   10. advance   11. payslip   12. bonus   13. payroll   14. package   15. weighting (for example, a job advertisement might offer an annual salary of $40000 + $5000 New York *weighting*)   16. leave (or *vacation*) entitlement   17. income / expenditure   18. satisfaction (often called *job satisfaction*)   19. commission   20. stock options   21. incentive plans   22. rate   23. redundancy pay   24. discount   25. relocation allowance   26. profit sharing   27. gross   28. net   29. index-linked   30. performance related   31. commensurate (for example, *Your salary will be commensurate with your experience and qualifications*)   32. golden handshake (some companies also give new employees a *golden hello* when they accept a job with the company)

Entertainment, art, sports and the media (pages 18 – 19)

(A) (The speaker is talking about a **newspaper** or a **current affairs magazine**) 1. circulation / readership   2. readership / circulation   3. coverage   4. events   5. features / articles   6. articles / features   7. researched   8. current   9. objective   10. lively   11. editor   12. journalists   13. Press
(B) (The speaker is talking about a **television news broadcast**) 1. technical   2. studio   3. anchor / reporter   4. reporter / anchor   5. off-screen   6. on air   7. live   8. network   9. complaints   10. broadcasting   11. break
(C) (The speaker is talking about a **novel**) 1. works   2. writer (*author* has a similar meaning)   3. literature   4. plot   5. character   6. set   7. action   8. biographical   9. recommend   10. issued   11. anthology   12. copy
(D) (The speaker is talking about a **movie**) 1. director   2. box-office   3. Award (an *Academy Award* is also known as an *Oscar*)   4. actors   5. performance   6. effects   7. scenery / cinematography   8. cinematography / scenery   9. soundtrack   10. critics   11. release (we can also say *nationwide release*)
(E) (The speaker is talking about a **play**) 1. opening (we can also say *first night*)   2. audience   3. curtain   4. lights   5. stage   6. half   7. performance (a 'part' of a play is called an *act,* so would also call the second half of a play the *second act*)   8. auditorium   9. cast (= *actors* in a film or play)   10. rehearsed   11. lines   12. dialog   13. scenery   14. backers   15. scriptwriter
(F) (The speaker is talking about a **museum**) 1. galleries   2. exhibits   3. ancient   4. acquired   5. collector (or collection)   6. art   7. collection   8. portraits   9. accomplished   10. artists   11. exhibitions   12. Admission   13. contribution (we could also say *donation*)
(G) (The speaker is talking about an **album** of **rock music**) 1. recordings   2. groups   3. note   4. track   5. fans / crowd   6. band   7. repertoire   8. hits   9. variations   10. studio   11. astute   12. crowd / fans   13. singer   14. compilation
(H) (The speaker is talking about a **sporting event** – in particular a **ball game** such as **soccer**) 1. supporters / spectators   2. stadium   3. players / teams   4. pitch   5. win   6. triumph / win   7. beat   8. opponents   9. captains   10. referee   11. cheerleaders   12. teams / players   13. spectators / supporters   14. coaches   15. encouragement   16. score   17. draw

Food and eating out (page 20)

1. (a) Customers / Diners (give yourself ½ point if you answered *Guests*)   (b) asked   (c) not   (d) restaurant   (e) want / would like   (f) g[
2. Food should not be *high* in cholesterol (1 point) It should be *low* in cholesterol (1 point). The best way of preparing meat and vegetabl[

67

Answers

is not by frying it (1 point): Steaming, boiling, and grilling (1 point for any of these words) are considered to be much healthier.

3. (a) goodness (or *vitamins* and *minerals*) (b) ingredients (c) rich in / high in (d) minimum (e) retain (we could also say *preserve*) (f) Wholesome (g) preparing (although you do not always need to *cook* food to prepare it) (h) free from (i) artificial (j) way

4. vegetarian / vegan / teetotaler

5. (a) to (b) on / of (c) down on / out (If you *cut down* on something you eat less of it. If you *cut out* something (from your diet) you stop eating it completely) (d) up (e) off (f) for / with

6. ranger = range / organism = organic / additions = additives / modification = modified / fat = fast (*fast food* is also sometimes called *junk food* because it is not very good for you)

7. recommend / reservation / service / waiting / portions / diet / undercooked / rare / well-done / burnt* / check / overcharged / service charge / tip (we can also use the more formal word *gratuity*)

*Meats such as steak and lamb are usually cooked *rare, medium-rare, medium, medium to well done* or *well-done*.

The maximum possible score in this quiz is 50 points. Add up your total score. If you scored over 40, well done! If you scored less than 30, look at the answers again, make a note of them, and try to review them on a regular basis so that they become a part of your 'active' vocabulary.

Hotels (pages 21 – 22)

1. rates 2. single 3. twin 4. double 5. occupancy 6. supplement 7. family 8. suite 9. en-suite 10. rates 11. quote 12. facilities 13. safety deposit 14. pay-to-view 15. Internet 16. amenities 17. residents 18. non-residents 19. room service 20. pool 21. business and conference 22. options 23. self-catering 24. bed and breakfast (B+B) 25. half-board 26. full-board 27. all-inclusive 28. peak period (we can also say *peak season*) 29. advance 30. reservations 31. vacancies 32. check-in 33. check-out 34. vacated 35. guests 36. charged 37. shuttle 38. transfer 39. chain 40. website 41. staff 42. experience 43. training 44. competitive 45. uniform 46. chambermaids 47. housekeeping 48. receptionists 49. waiters / waitresses 50. waitresses / waiters (note that we often say *waiting staff* for men and women) 51. chefs 52. cashiers

Job advertising (pages 23 – 24)

Exercise 1:

1. G 2. S 3. O 4. N 5. X 6. I 7. T 8. B 9. F 10. W 11. L 12. D 13. V 14. Q 15. U 16. C 17. J 18. A 19. R 20. E 21. K 22. H 23. P 24. M

Exercise 2:

1. leading 2. vacancy 3. post (we can also say *position* or *job*) 4. commencing 5. application (the verb is *to apply*) 6. candidate (we can also say *applicant*) 7. qualified 8. experience 9. team 10. drive 11. motivate (the noun is *motivation*, the adjective is *motivated*) 12. colleagues (we sometimes use the informal word *workmates*) 13. responsibilities (we can also say *duties*) 14. rewards package (we can also say *benefits package*) 15. basic salary (note that a *salary* is the money, or *pay*, you receive every <u>month</u> or <u>year</u> for doing your job; a *wage* is money you receive every <u>day</u> or <u>week</u> for doing a job: see the section on *Earnings, rewards and benefits* elsewhere in this book for more information) 16. commission 17. incentive 18. increment 19. relocation allowance 20. benefits (we can also say *rewards*) 21. advance 22. résumé (sometimes called a *curriculum vitae*, or *CV*, in British English. A résumé lists your qualifications and experience in detail, and also provides important personal information – name, age, contact details, etc.) 23. covering letter 24. interview (A person <u>attending</u> an interview is called an *interviewee*; a person <u>conducting</u> an interview is called an *interviewer*)

Job recruitment (pages 25 – 26)

Part 1

1. vacancy 2. hire or recruit 3. staff 4. advertises 5. post or position 6. internally 7. externally 8. agency 9. work (job is countable, and should be preceded by an article or pronoun) 10. description 11. applicant 12. applying 13. requirements 14. qualifications 15. experience 16. qualities (we can also say *attributes*) 17. practical 18. professional 19. rewards or remuneration 20. salary (a *wage* is paid daily or weekly) 21. rises / increments (with a slight difference in meaning: a pay *rise* might be the result of promotion or hard work, an *increment* is usually automatic and based on length of time with the company.) 22. benefits 23. leave or vacations (leave is more formal) 24. package (we often use the expression a *rewards and benefits package*) 25. commensurate

Part 2

1. résumé (this is a French word, so it is considered more correct to put the accent on both e's) 2. cover (in American English) covering (in British English) 3. fill in or fill out (we can also say *complete*) 4. application 5. submit or send (*submit* is more formal) 6. short-list 7. attend 8. reject or turn down 9. unsuitable 10. candidates or applicants 11. potential 12. appearance 13. disposition 14. skills or abilities 15. interests or hobbies 16. background (we can also say *circumstances*) 17. medical 18. suits or matches (although *matches* is the best word) 19. profile or criteria 20. offered 21. references (the *referees* in this situation are the people who write the references) 22. employer (although if you have come from a managerial position in another company, one of your employees might be asked to say what you are like as a manager) 23. colleague or co-worker (we can also use the less-formal *workmate*) 24. induction 25. temporary 26. trial or probationary 27. permanent 28. appraisal

For reference see *Easier English Intermediate Dictionary* (0-7475-6989-4).

Joining ideas together: addition, equation and conclusion (page 27)

1. B, C, D (*Therefore* cannot be used because the second sentence is not a result of the first) 2. A, C, D   3. A, B, D (*Along with* needs to be followed by a noun or an -ing verb) 4. A, D (*Likewise* cannot be used because the second sentence is a result of the first sentence. *Because of* needs to be followed by a noun or adjective + noun: *Because of a drop in sales, we had to close the department down*) 5. A (*In brief* is used to summarize what the speaker thinks, and usually follows a list of facts) 6. C (*Together* would also be correct if it was followed by *with*: ...*together with half the sales staff*) 7. A, B (the second sentence is a result of the first sentence) 8. A, B, C, D (these expressions are usually followed by a noun or an adjective + noun) 9. D (an informal expression, which you would normally only use in spoken English) 10. A, B (*also* is usually used before a verb and is not usually used at the end of a sentence) 11. A, C (*However* and *Nevertheless* are not usually used before a verb) 12. A, D (The second sentence recommends action as a result of the first sentence)

Location and direction (pages 28 – 29)

Language relating to location and direction is particularly useful if you take the TOEIC Test of Spoken English, where you may be required to describe where places are on a map, and explain how to get to them.

A. City Hall   B. Easy Street   C. fast food restaurant   D. nightclub   **E. The movie theater**   F. Park lane   G. Central Avenue   H. Telegraph Road   I. deli   J. tourist information office   K. railway station   L. bus station   M. Stallone Street   N. library   O. Commercial Street   P. department store   Q. post office   R. museum   S. Luigi's restaurant   T. art gallery   U. Grand Hotel   V. Clemenceau Avenue   W. Washington Park   X. Dominion Street   Y. shopping Mall   Z. Marlene's bar

Meetings and presentations (page 30)

1. open   2. welcoming   3. participants   4. attendance   5. supporting   6. agenda   7. progress   8. schedule   9. get through   10. achieve   11. goals   12. objectives   13. chair (we can also say preside over)   14. contribute   15. clarification   16. interrupt   17. issues   18. address (= discuss / talk about)   19. bringing up   20. matters   21. priority   22. summarizing   23. points   24. recommendations   25. open floor   26. opinions   27. closes   28. notes   29. minutes   30. report   31. complaints   32. questions   33. floor

Money matters 1 (page 31)

Exercise 1:
1. If you **lend** money, you let someone use your money for a certain period of time. If you **borrow** money, you take someone's money for a short time (usually paying *interest* – see number 19) and then repay it. (Note that you *lend* money <u>to</u> someone, and you *borrow* money <u>from</u> someone).
2. **Inflation** is a state of economy where prices and wages increase (= *go up*). **Deflation** is a reduction of economic activity.
3. A **discount** is the percentage by which a full price is reduced in a shop (if the reduction is very big, we can say that it is a *bargain*). A **refund** is money paid when, for example, returning something to a shop (you will normally need to show a *receipt* when getting a refund – see number 8). Note that *refund* can also be a verb: *to refund money*.
4. **Income** is the money you receive (your *wage* or *salary* is part of your income). **Expenditure** is money you spend. Most people would like their income to be greater than their expenditure.
5. If a company is **insolvent**, it has lost all its money. If a company is **bankrupt**, it has lost all its money , it has also borrowed a lot, and it cannot pay back its *debts* (= money it owes). Being bankrupt is a very serious financial situation for a company to be in. (Note that a company <u>goes</u> bankrupt, or is <u>declared</u> bankrupt in a court of law. *Bankrupt* can also be a verb: *the current economic situation has bankrupted us*)
6. A bank **statement** is a detailed written document from a bank showing how much money has gone into and come out of a bank account. A **balance** is the amount of money you have in your bank account.
7. If your bank account is **in the red**, your *expenditure* has been greater than your *income* (see number 4), and so you have less than $0 in your bank account. If your account is **in the black**, you have more than $0 in your bank account.
8. An **invoice** is a note, or *bill*, sent to you to ask for payment for goods or services (it can also be a verb: *to invoice* someone for something). A **receipt** is a note (from a shop, for example) which shows how much you have paid for something.
9. When you make a **profit**, you gain money from selling something which is more than the money you paid for it. When you make a **loss**, you have spent money which you have not gotten back.
10. **Gross** profit is the profit you make *before* money is taken away to cover costs of production, labor, tax, etc. **Net** profit is the money you are left with *after* costs, taxes, etc., have been taken away (money which is taken away is called a *deduction*).
11. If you have been **undercharged**, you have paid less than you should have for goods or services. If you have been **overcharged**, you have paid too much.
12. Something which is **overpriced** is too expensive. Something which is **exorbitant** costs much more than its true value (we can also use the more informal word *extortionate*).
13. If you **save** money, you keep it so that you can use it later. If you **invest** money, you put it into property, stocks, etc., so that it will increase in value (the noun is *investment*).
14. A **wage** and a **salary** are both money you receive for doing a job, but a wage is usually paid *daily* or *weekly* and a salary is usually paid *monthly*.
15. **Extravagant** describes someone who spends a lot of money. **Economical** (= *frugal*) describes someone who is careful with money.
16. A **loan** is money that you borrow to buy something. A **mortgage** is a special kind of loan used to buy a house or other building over a period of time.
17. A **loan** is money you borrow from a bank, and a formal arrangement has been made with the bank for this. An **overdraft** is the

For reference see *Easier English Intermediate Dictionary* (0-7475-6989-4).

Answers

amount of money you withdraw from your bank, which is more than there is your account. It is usually done *without* making an arrangement with the bank (although many banks offer their customers automatic *overdraft facilities*).

18. A **share** is one of the many equal parts into which a company's *capital* (= money that is invested in the company) is divided. People who buy them are called *shareholders*. A **stock** is an investment in a company represented by shares. (Note that in the United Kingdom, stocks are shares which are issued by the government).

19. **Commission** is the percentage of sales value given to a sales person in a company. **Interest** is the percentage that is paid to someone for lending money.

20. A **worthless** (= *valueless*) object is something which has no value. A **priceless** object is an extremely valuable object.

21. When you **credit** an account, you put money into it. When you **debit** an account, you take money out of it.

22. A **pension** is the money that someone continues to receive after they have retired from a job. **Redundancy pay** is the money that is given to someone to compensate then for losing their job when a company makes them *redundant* (= no longer needed). (Note that if you lose your job and cannot find another one, you can receive *welfare* (= money from the government)).

23. A **dividend** is part of a company's profits shared out among shareholders (see number 18). A **royalty** is money paid to the author of a book, an actor, a rock star, etc., as a percentage of sales (it is usually plural: *Royalties are paid twice each year*).

24. **Tax** is money taken by the government from incomes, sales, etc., to pay for government services. **Duty** is a special tax that has to be paid for bringing goods into a country (it is often called *import duty*).

25. If you **deposit** money in an account, you put money into the account. If you **withdraw** money, you take it out of your account.

26. A **bill** is a piece of paper showing the amount of money that you have to pay for goods or services (for example, an electricity bill). A **check** is a bill that you receive in a restaurant.

Exercise 2:
1. refund / receipt   2. overcharged / check / tax / exorbitant   3. statement *or* balance / overdraft / in the red / expenditure   4. gross / salary / commission / net / income *or* salary   5. bankrupt / redundancy pay / pension / invested / stocks *or* shares / worthless

Money matters 2 (pages 32 – 33)

1. afford   2. check   3. owes   4. deducted   5. rebate   6. credit   7. bargains (we can also say *offers* or *reductions*)   8. welfare
9. cost   10. funding   11. currency   12. finances   13. assets   14. compensation   15. capital   16. subsidized   17. sponsored
18. yield (we can also say *returns* or *dividends*)   19. profitable (we can also say *lucrative*)   20. earnings   21. fortune   22. down payment (we can also say *deposit* or advance payment)   23. budget   24. audit   25. debts   26. charge   27. rate   28. currency

See the opposite page for how the completed crossword grid should look.

For reference see *Easier English Intermediate Dictionary* (0-7475-6989-4).

Obligation and option (page 34)

1. required (not *mandatory* or *compulsory*, as these cannot be followed with *by*)   2. compulsory (*mandatory* could also be used if the helmet and equipment must be worn because of a law)   3. must (not *have*, as this must be followed with *to*)   4. have / need   5. liable (not *obliged* or *compelled*, as these must be followed with *to*)   6. forced (this is better than *obliged* or *compelled*, as it is stronger and suggests that the company has no other choice. Also, *obliged* and *compelled* are usually used when somebody makes somebody else do something)   7. exempt   8. Mandatory (this is better than *Compulsory*, as it suggests the checks must be carried out because of a law: see 2 above)   9. voluntary (not *optional*, as the gap is preceded by *a*, not *an*)   10. optional (not *voluntary*, as the gap is preceded by *an*) 11. alternative (used as part of an expression: *We have no alternative but to…*)   12. obliged / required   13. obligation (note the adjective form of obliged / obligation = *obligatory*)   14. compelled (in other words, he felt that people were putting pressure on him to make him leave. We could also use *obliged*)   15. entail (we can also say *involve*)   16. need (use here as a noun)   17. essential (*vital* or *imperative* could also be used)

Answers

<u>Opposites 1: verbs and adjectives (page 35)</u>

1. succeed   2. hollow   3. permanent   4. sharp   5. punish   6. public   7. smooth   8. approximate   9. borrow   10. guilty
11. advance   12. minor   13. shallow   14. amateur   15. present   16. artificial   17. accept   18. destroy   19. deny

The words in the shaded vertical strip are *compulsory* (= *obligatory*) and *voluntary*.

<u>Opposites 2: adjective prefixes (page 36)</u>

<u>Task 1</u>:
unacceptable   inaccurate   inadequate   disadvantaged   disagreeable   unattractive   unauthorized   unavoidable   unbelievable
uncertain   uncomfortable   incompetent   incomplete   unconscious   discontented   unconvincing   incorrect   incurable   uneven
unfair   unfashionable   dishonest   disinclined   illegal   unlimited   illiterate   illogical   unmarried   immature   immoral   immortal
disobedient   disorganized   impatient   imperfect   impersonal   impossible   improper   impure   unqualified (<u>disqualified</u> is a verb
which means to make someone not able to do something: *He was disqualified from driving for a year*)   irrational   irregular   irrelevant
irreplaceable   irresistible   irresolute   irresponsible   unsatisfactory   dissatisfied   insufficient   unwelcome

Note that adjectives which end with *-ful* are usually made into their opposite form by changing *-ful* to *-less* (*thoughtful* = *thoughtless*,
useful = *useless*, etc.). Helpful is one exception to this rule (the opposite is *unhelpful*. *Help<u>less</u>* has a different meaning, and means not able
to do anything)

<u>Task 2</u>:
1. D (= disinclined)   2. B (= dishonest)   3. C (= insufficient)   4. A (= irresponsible)   5. C (= unconvincing)   6. A (= inadequate)

<u>Opposites 3: verb prefixes (pages 37 – 38)</u>

<u>Across</u>: 2. misquoted   3. misdiagnosing   6. discontinuing   8. misrepresent   10. unloaded   12. disagrees   13. misuses   14. unlock
16. unfolded   20. distrust or mistrust   22. disapproves   23. disobeyed
<u>Down</u>: 1. misjudged   2. misunderstands   4. disconnecting   5. disqualified   7. displeased   9. miscalculated   11. misbehave
15. disallowed   17. misplaced   18. uncovered (not *discovered*)   19. disproved   21. dislike

<u>Ownership, giving, lending and borrowing (page 39)</u>

1. Property   2. landlords   3. allocated   4. provided   5. mortgage   6. donation (the verb is to *donate*)   7. possessions   8. tenants
9. loan (this can also be a verb: *to loan*)   10. contribute   11. leased (the noun is *lease*: *to sign a lease*)

The word in the shaded vertical strip is *proprietors* (= owners of a business)

<u>Phrasal verbs 1 (page 40)</u>

1. go up   2. end up   3. cut off   4. fill out (*fill in* has the same meaning)   5. run out of   6. called off   7. do away with   8. subjected
to   9. get through to   10. come up against   11. pulling through   12. went through with   13. looking forward to

<u>Phrasal verbs 2 (page 41)</u>

1. on   2. out   3. up   4. off   5. over   6. down   7. in   8. up   9. into   10. up with

<u>Phrasal verbs 3 (page 42)</u>

1. going up = going through   2. checking into = checking in (you *check into* a hotel, but you *check in* for a flight)   3. come up to = come
up with   4. build about = build up   5. fall up = fall through   6. bring apart = bring together   7. dropping in of = dropping out of
8. falls for = falls to   9. coming through with = coming down with   10. came in = came into   11. takes to = takes after   12. turn round
= turn up

<u>Prepositions 1 (page 43)</u>

1. on* (note that the date in sentence 1 is spoken '*the second of April*' or '*April the second*')   2. by (= no later than)   3. since   4. under
5. across (*around* could also be used in this sentence)   6. with   7. to   8. for   9. out (*away* could also be used in this sentence)
10. from   11. on   12. to   13. from   14. in   15. by   16. by   17. for   18. through (*for* and *throughout* could also be used in this
sentence)   19. in   20. in

* When we talk about times and dates: *on* is used for days and specific dates (*on Monday* / *on September 15* / *on Monday September 15*);
in is used for months, years, seasons and periods of the day (*in September* / *in 2005* / *in summer* / *in the evening*); *at* is used for specific
times (*at 7.30 p.m.*).

The correct preposition is shown in brackets.
1. B (on)   2. A (between)   3. B (for)   4. C (under)   5. D (on)   6. C (until *or* before)   7. D (through)   8. C (on)   9. A (by)   10. D (from)   11. B (for)   12. C (of)   13. D (with)   14. C (in)

Sales and Marketing (pages 45 – 46)

Exercise 1:
1. cowded = crowded   2. nich = niche   3. brocure = brochure   4. opmarket = upmarket   5. reserch = research   6. advertiseing = advertising   7. campain = campaign   8. premote = promote   9. comercials = commercials   10. advertisments = advertisements   11. billyboards = billboards   12. plop-ups = pop-ups   13. mailshoots = mailshots   14. sponsership = sponsorship   15. endoarse = endorse   16. pont = point   17. retale = retail   18. pich = pitch   19. disconts = discounts   20. giveways = giveaways   21. dommestic = domestic   22. expot = export   23. raps = reps (a short form of sales representatives)   24. franshise = franchise   25. merchantising = merchandising   26. brant = brand   27. pakaging = packaging   28. cattalog = catalog (or *catalogue*)   29. hyp = hype   30. fat = fad   31. competiton = competition   32. canvince = convince   33. perswading = persuading

Exercise 2:
1. catalog (or *brochure*)   2. endorse   3. packaging   4. point of sale   5. pitch   6. fad   7. hype   8. competition   9. brand (often called *branded goods*)   10. discount   11. sponsorship   12. mailshot   13. upmarket (the opposite is *downmarket*)   14. export

Shopping and consumerism (pages 47 – 48)

1. (A) concessions (we can also say *franchises*)   (B) chain   2. (A) customers   (B) consumer   3. (A) charging   (B) cost   4. (A) spend (you *spend* money *on* something)   (B) paid (you *pay* money *for* something)   5. (A) credit   (B) debited   6. (A) discount   (B) offer (we can also say *bargain*)   7. (A) change   (B) exchange   8. (A) prices   (B) costs (also often called *overhead*)   9. (A) wholesale (we can also say *in bulk*. You *make a bulk purchase* of something)   (B) retail   10. (A) for sale   (B) on sale   11. (A) receipt   (B) bills   12. (A) check   (B) bill (note the difference in meaning of *bill* in 11 and 12)   13. (A) check (note the difference in meaning of *check* in 12 and 13. Also note that you usually only ask for a check in a restaurant or bar)   (B) charge (a *charge card* is also called a *credit card*)   14. (A) economical   (B) economic   15. (A) stock   (B) supply   16. (A) served   (B) service   17. (A) demand   (B) supply   18. (A) merchandise   (B) purchases   19. (A) refund   (B) return   20. (A) staff   (B) team   21. (A) do (note that people *go shopping* or they *do their shopping*)   (B) made

Similar meanings 1: nouns (pages 49 – 51)

Exercise 1:
1. agenda / schedule   2. accommodation / housing   3. discipline / order   4. assistance / help   5. drop / decline (*fall* could also be used)   6. faults / defects   7. opposition / resistance   8. proof / evidence   9. discount / reduction   10. proximity / closeness   11. appointment / meeting   12. customers / clients   13. work / employment   14. benefits / advantages   15. requirements / prerequisites

Exercise 2:
1. acclaim / praise   2. code / rules   3. liability / responsibility   4. choices / options   5. overview / (short) description   6. staff / personnel (*employees* could also be used)   7. cooperation / collaboration   8. Customers / Patrons   9. terms / conditions (often used as one expression: *the terms and conditions of the contract*)   10. questions / queries   11. outlets (often called *retail outlets*) / stores   12. problems / complications   13. strategy / plan   14. priority / precedence   15. revisions / changes

Exercise 3:
1. reviews / write-ups   2. advertising / publicity   3. charisma / (personal) appeal   4. categories / classifications   5. ending / termination   6. entitlement / right   7. caliber / intellect and ability   8. specialist / expert   9. assignment / job   10. notion / idea   11. proficiency / skill   12. achievement / accomplishment   13. ultimatum / final demand   14. disparity / difference   15. proceeds / earnings

Similar meanings 2: verbs (pages 52 – 53)

Across:
1. audit   2. explain   5. reclaim   6. promote   9. assist   11. exhaust   15. assert   17. avert   18. dictate   19. obtain   21. influence   22. administer   24. generate   25. select   27. realize   29. relate   31. measure   34. ban   35. brief   36. verify   38. increase   40. consult   41. endorse   42. require   43. convey   44. deduct

Down:
1. address   2. employ   3. award   4. disturb   7. ascertain   8. gather   10. substitute   12. accelerate   13. handle   14. regulate   16. attend   20. compensate   23. reserve   26. retain   28. imply   29. reveal   30. clarify   32. analyze   33. resolve   37. finalize   39. consent

Note that using a word with a similar meaning to another word does not always mean using that word in exactly the same way structurally or lexically. For example: you can '*prevent a strike from taking place*' or you can '*avert a strike*' (not '*avert a strike from taking place*'); you can '*suggest something without saying it directly*' or you can '*imply something*' (not '*imply something without saying it directly*'). In these examples, the words at the end are not necessary because their meaning is carried in the main verb. This is one reason why you should always record words in context, and with an example that shows how they are used, so that when you use them yourself, you use them correctly.

For reference see *Easier English Intermediate Dictionary* (0-7475-6989-4).

Answers

Also note that some of these verbs can be used in more than one way. For example, you can <u>convey</u> *a message to someone*, or you can <u>convey</u> *goods from one place to another*.

<u>Similar meanings 3: adjectives (page 54)</u>

<u>Exercise 1:</u>
1. mandatory   2. integral   3. efficient   4. compatible   5. obligatory   6. lengthy   7. inventive   8. important   9. disparate
10. prosperous   11. legitimate   12. voluntary   13. steady   14. exceptional   15. diverse   16. flexible   17. profitable   18. disciplinary
19. tedious   20. punctual   21. nominal   22. perceptive   23. modern   24. industrious

<u>Exercise 2:</u>
1. vibrant   2. simple   3. resolute   4. luxurious   5. prospective   6. restricted   7. thriving   8. enduring   9. extensive   10. rudimentary
11. relevant   12. adequate   13. abrupt   14. outdated   15. overall   16. risky   17. abundant   18. narrow   19. inconsistent
20. inflexible   21. crucial   22. thorough   23. discourteous   24. scrupulous

<u>Starting and stopping (pages 55 – 56)</u>

1. terminated *or* canceled   2. deleted   3. backed out *or* pulled out   4. outbreak   5. set up *or* established / shut down   6. embarking *or* setting off   7. suppress *or* quash   8. eradicated   9. deter   10. dissuade / initiated   11. launched / take off   12. suspended
13. took up   14. phased in / phased out   15. inception / closure   16. ceased   17. retiring   18. quit (= informal) *or* resign / fired (= informal) or dismissed   19. turn…down   20. freeze   21. discontinued   22. abolished   23. kick off (= informal)   24. arisen

<u>Travel 1 (pages 57 – 58)</u>

<u>Exercise 1:</u>
1. abroad   2. vacation (note that in British English, people say *holiday*. A holiday in American English is a day when people do not have to go to work: for example, Thanksgiving, Labor Day, etc.)   3. mass   4. package   5. transfers   6. accommodations (note that in British English, *accommodations* can also be singular: *accommodation*)   7. travel agency (we can also say *travel agent's*. A *travel operator*, or *tour operator*, is a company that arranges tours and usually sells them through a travel agency)   8. brochure   9. destination   10. itinerary
11. both words can be used, but *book* is more common   12. both expressions are correct   13. both words are correct   14. both words are correct (*depart* is more formal)   15. independent   16. flexibility   17. departure   18. airfare   19. e-ticket   20. both words are correct   21. confirmation (from the verb *to confirm*)   22. trip (an excursion is usually a day trip somewhere as part of a vacation)
23. check in (*check-in* is a noun or adjective: *He arrived at the <u>check-in</u> five minutes too late / Go to the <u>check-in</u> desk two hours before your flight*)   24. terminal (a *terminus* is a place where a train or bus ends its journey)   25. Ticketless   26. valid   27. both are correct (*expires* is more formal)   28. visa (note that there are different types of visa, including *entry visas*, *transit visas*, *work visas*, etc.)
29. embassy   30. traveler's checks   31. currency   32. exchange   33. deal (*bargain* sounds strange when preceded by *favorable*)
34. commission   35. insurance   36. vaccinations (The verb is *to vaccinate*. We can also say *inoculations* or *immunizations*)   37. arrangements

<u>Exercise 2:</u>
1. independent   2. e-ticket   3. airfare   4. abroad   5. mass   6. commission   7. exchange   8. vaccination   9. terminal   10. package
11. check in   12. valid   13. booking / reservation   14. trip   15. confirmation

<u>Travel 2 (page 59)</u>

1. delayed   2. overbooked   3. tourist / coach (*economy* is used in British English)   4. embarkation / boarding   5. transit   6. domestic (we can also say *internal* for flights that go between airports in the same country)   7. round-trip (= *return* in British English. A *one-way ticket* is called a *single* in British English)   8. credit limit   9. crew (although *team* might also be used as a more informal alternative)
10. commuters (note that a *mile* is a measurement of distance equivalent to 1.61 kilometers)   11. carrier / airline   12. comprehensive
13. All of these are correct (although *eco-tourism* and *environmental tourism* often involve the tourist in actually doing something to help the environment while he / she is in the host country)   14. SUV (= *sport utility vehicle*, often called an *off-roader*, or a *4X4 (four by four)* in British English)

For reference see *Easier English Intermediate Dictionary* (0-7475-6989-4).

Exercise 1:

Remove 2 letters, then add 4 letters:	provide = provision persuade = persuasion recognize = recognition abolish = abolition decide = decision
Remove 1 letter, then add 7 letters:	qualify = qualification apply = application identify = identification notify = notification imply = implication
Remove 1 letter, then add 5 letters:	consume = consumption admire = admiration permit = permission determine = determination compete = competition
Remove 1 letter, then add 4 letters:	argue = argument assure = assurance intervene = intervention expand = expansion produce = production
Remove 1 letter, then add 3 letters:	negotiate = negotiation expose = exposure supervise = supervision (*supervisor*, a person who supervises, could also go in the section below) behave = behavior promote = promotion
Remove 1 letter, then add 2 letters:	refuse = refusal survive = survival (or survivor, somebody who survives) arrive = arrival rehearse = rehearsal respond = response
Add 3 letters:	fail = failure coincide = coincidence warn = warning suggest = suggestion prohibit = prohibition
Add 4 letters:	disturb = disturbance attend = attendance require = requirement manage = management (a manager is somebody who manages, eg, a company or department) prefer = preference
Add 5 letters:	sign = signature expect = expectation recommend = recommendation consult = consultation relax = relaxation

Exercise 2:

1. choice (from *choose*)   2. solution (from *solve*)   3. emphasis (from *emphasize*)   4. subscription (from *subscribe*)   5. scrutiny (from *scrutinize*)   6. justification (from *justify*)   7. criticism (from *criticize*)   8. acquisition (from *acquire*)   9. loss (from *lose*)   10. maintenance (from *maintain*)

The verb / noun in the shaded strip is *compromise*.

Word forms 2: nouns from adjectives (pages 62 – 63)

Exercise 1:
1. value   2. ✓   3. thirst   4. honesty   5. ✓   6. expense   7. ✓   8. similarities   9. certainty   10. absenteeism (or absence)   11. convenience   12. necessity   13. ✓   14. flexibility   15. ✓   16. responsibility   17. accuracy   18. ✓   19. complications   20. difference

For reference see *Easier English Intermediate Dictionary* (0-7475-6989-4).

Answers

Remove 4 letters:	comfortable = comfort fashionable = fashion systematic = system
Remove 3 letters, then add 5 letters:	long = length high = height strong = strength
Remove 3 letters, then add 1 letter:	optimistic = optimism pessimistic = pessimism realistic = realism (*reality* is also a noun form)
Remove 2 letters, then add 5 letters:	able = ability available = availability compatible = compatibility
Remove 2 letters, then add 3 letters:	hot = heat deep = depth confused = confusion
Remove 2 letters, then add 2 letters:	aggressive = aggression creative = creation appreciative = appreciation
Remove 2 letters:	functional = function logical = logic optional = option
Remove 1 letter, then add 3 letters:	considerate = consideration mature = maturity secure = security
Remove 1 letter, then add 2 letters:	convenient = convenience sufficient = sufficiency true = truth
Add 2 letters:	bored = boredom loyal = loyalty warm = warmth
Add 3 letters:	familiar = familiarity popular = popularity punctual = punctuality
Add 4 letters:	aware = awareness serious = seriousness weak = weakness

Word forms 3: adjectives from verbs (page 64)

1. promotional / inspiring   2. innovative / impressive   3. wasteful / obligatory   4. repetitive / boring   5. excited / doubtful   6. decisive / active   7. inventive / changeable   8. continual (= stopping and starting) / continuous (without stopping)   9. approachable / frightening   10. convincing / critical   11. inclusive / competitive   12. helpful / supportive / dependable   13. rectifiable / preferable   14. negotiable / refundable   15. restricted / valid   16. voluntary / constructive   17. avoidable / careless (not *careful*)   18. creative / imaginative / admirable   19. specific / occupational   20. attractive / excellent

Workplace problems (page 65)

Paragraph (A)
1. dispute   2. resolved   3. strike   4. arbitrate

Paragraph (B)
1. timekeeping   2. absenteeism   3. misconduct

Paragraph (C)
1. fraud   2. discrimination   3. bullying   4. racial   5. abuse   6. sexual   7. harassment   8. fired   9. suspended   10. unfair   11. dismissal (we can also say *wrongful dismissal*)   12. appeal

Paragraph (D)
1. breaches   2. neglecting (this can also be a noun: *neglect* of duties)   3. insubordination   4. damage   5. disciplinary   6. board   7. instant   8. dismissal

Paragraph (E)
1. shortages   2. overstretched   3. grievance (= a formal word for *complaint*)   4. walkout   5. verbal   6. warning (after a *verbal warning*, an employee might receive a *written warning*)   7. notice (when a company *asks you for your notice*, they are politely telling you that they are going to force you to resign)

Paragraph (F)
1. dropped   2. redundant   3. resigned   4. bankrupt   5. hacked   6. virus   7. crashed   8. order (*out of order* = broken / not working)

For reference see *Easier English Intermediate Dictionary* (0-7475-6989-4).